Acknowledgement

I have been fortunate to work and
wonderful people who have shape

Top of the list must go my leadership team at Clicktools. Much of what
is written here was the result of our work, our challenges and, not
least, our arguments. Thanks to Andrew Chapman, Steve Mountfield,
Nick Taylor and Andrew Walker. After selling half of Clicktools to
Survey Monkey, I was fortunate to learn from Brent Chudoba, Damon
Cronkey and Tim Maly, all of whom served as Non-Executive Directors.
I only wish the late, great Dave Goldberg (former CEO of Survey
Monkey) was still alive to hear my heartfelt thanks for all the times he
asked me, "How can I help you?" In a similar vein, I learned much
from Leslie Stretch and Rory Cameron (to whom my wife gave the
moniker "my dangerous friend") at Callidus following their acquisition
of Clicktools.

The CS community is great at sharing ideas and experiences, and the
list of people who have helped and shaped my thinking would fill a
book. That said, there are a few people who went over and above in
their support for me. Shreesha Ramdas has always provided
inspiration and been available when I needed help and support, as has
Dan Steinman. I met Dan Steinman when he moved to London; we
shared ideas, speaking platforms and a couple of beers on several
occasions. He inspired me to think more deeply about customer
success. Rav Dhaliwal is the reason this book is months later than
expected. He shared his views and helped me think through a few of
the ideas. Most importantly, he convinced me I should change my
audience and focus from CS leaders to SaaS CEOs.

One community above all deserves recognition, thanks and
appreciation. The hundreds of people who I have been privileged to
call customers. This book is about them, for them and inspired by
them.

Thank you to all of you.

PART ONE

Scene setting and concepts

In this section I explain the history of SaaS, the changes that are shaping it There's also a brief philosophical rant about how we think about organisation.

1: How we got to here

It started with churn

Whilst the history of SaaS is short, I think it would be helpful to review briefly what led us to where we are now.

The move to SaaS delivery and subscription-based pricing influenced a number of changes. New suppliers entered the market with products at lower price points, and annual or even monthly contracts created significantly lower initial costs. This reduced massively the financial risk of investing in new software. This coincided with and contributed to a shift from selling to IT to engaging business managers as the primary buyer. Simpler infrastructure, lower costs and short-term contracts also made switching suppliers easier, creating the potential problem of churn. It is this churn challenge, their Doctor Doom moment, that often drives CEOs to turn to customer success.

It was into this environment that Gainsight published their seminal book *Customer Success*[6] and introduced the ten laws:

1. Sell to the right customers;
2. The natural tendency is for customers and vendors to drift apart;
3. Customers expect you to make them wildly successful;
4. Relentlessly monitor and manage customer health;
5. You can no longer build loyalty through personal relationships;
6. Product is your only scalable differentiator;

---

[6] **Customer Success**: How Innovative Companies Are Reducing Churn and Growing Recurring Revenue by Mehta, Nick; Steinman, Dan; Murphy, Lincoln.

7. Obsessively improve time to value;
8. Deeply understand your customer metrics;
9. Drive customer success through hard metrics;
10. It's a top down, company-wide commitment.

The most significant contribution was to place focus on the reasons B2B customers buy, i.e. to help them address a challenge or opportunity. Helping them to achieve this is, therefore, the primary key to continued business and the raison d'être for what is now called customer success.

Saying–doing gaps

Despite the excellent advice provided in the ten laws, and even more in numerous online forums, webinars and conferences, current practice in many B2B SaaS companies is lacking. What is said all too often falls short of what the majority of companies do. That is not to say there are no examples of companies doing great things, nor that what is being done is damaging. I do, however, contend that many CEOs – and, therefore, their customers – are not getting the return their efforts deserve. There are a number of gaps between what is said and what is done that hold companies back. These are the most significant gaps that I perceive.

Lack of deep customer understanding

"*It does what says on the tin*" is an advertising slogan[7] that should apply to customer success. The very words "customer success" say it all: it's about making the customer successful. This is only possible if the company has a **deep** understanding of its chosen customers. You cannot deliver success to customers if you do not understand who they are and what they are seeking to achieve – their problems and challenges.

---

[7] Used by the UK manufacturer of the Ronseal range of products

As the first of the original ten laws rightly states: "Sell to the right customers". Many companies fail to define their target customers in sufficient detail, and even those that do often fail to follow through. The pressure to hit a sales number leads to the acquisition of customers where the company will struggle to deliver success to the customer. I recall one CEO telling me that very high first-quarter churn was an issue, but the revenue generated exceeded the cost of acquisition so it was better than not making the sale. No thought to the time the salesperson could have spent on winning a good fit customer or the cost of servicing that customer (bad fit customers are almost always a resource black hole), let alone the massive damage to the company's reputation caused by highly disgruntled customers.

It's not just about the company. Deep understanding includes the characteristics of key people: users, key influencers and decision makers. These are the people that will determine if success has been achieved. You cannot claim to be focused on customer success if you do not know how they understand and measure success and what help they need to achieve it. It is the very foundation of customer success but an area where too many companies pay lip service.

Those that understand their chosen customers better than the competition have a real opportunity to gain a competitive advantage. You underinvest in building and, just as important, maintaining that deep customer understanding at your peril.

Product adoption not customer value

One important manifestation of the lack of customer understanding is a focus on the product alone. Some might say this is an odd comment given that B2B SaaS companies sell products. Remember, however, that you started your company because you identified a way to help customers to better solve a problem or capitalise on an opportunity. Resolution of that problem or opportunity, the outcome or goal, is the very reason you built a SaaS product. But here's the rub: technology alone rarely solves a problem. Processes, metrics, skills, even behaviours may also have to change to achieve the goal. Getting a customer to use your product(s) effectively is one element of the customer achieving their goal, but it is rarely sufficient on its own. This is not a new revelation: it has been talked about in technology since day one. Despite this being widely acknowledged, too many suppliers stop at adoption with the advice and guidance they provide.

This product focus is evident in many so-called customer success plans: the steps suppliers put in place for new customers. The early stages of training and adoption are detailed and well thought out. Thereafter, in the majority of cases, the rigour and detail diminish. These early steps are important. First impressions count, and it is vital to maintain the momentum and commitment created in the sales process. Failing to apply the same rigour beyond this initial phase is a bit like declaring yourself the winner after crossing the line first on the first lap of a 1500m race.

This gap still exists in too many companies. A meeting of CS leaders in the Bay Area in January 2020 highlighted ten trends for customer success, the last of which was "More focus on customer outcomes". Enough said.

Measuring the wrong things

A metrics related survey[8] asked SaaS companies how they measure customer success. They responded:

- Net Promoter Score (NPS) 85%;
- Annual/Monthly Recurring Revenue (ARR/MRR) 56%;
- Retention/Churn 53%;
- Revenue Growth 46%.

All these KPIs share one characteristic: they have nothing to do with how successful your customer is. They are all measures of your company's success. That's not to say they are unimportant – they are vital for understanding your company's performance – but they don't

---

[8] A Strikedeck/Service XRG study of over 300 CS professionals reported Oct 2019.

measure what it says on the tin. They are also all lagging indicators and don't help in understanding drivers of either the customers' success or the company's financial performance.

The premise of customer success, its very essence, is that achieving value, in the way the customer understands it, is a significant driver of customer retention, expansion and advocacy. If this is true, and I believe it is, then it has to be measured. If you are not measuring your customer's success, how can you claim to be doing customer success? Some claim that by measuring customer health they are tracking customer success. The problem with health scores is that few include any reference to or proxies that correlate with customers achieving their goals. Many of the health scores I have seen fail the success for customers test. In Chapter Seven, I will introduce the Value Framework, a method of relating the needs of key customer stakeholders to value metrics and the way your product helps them achieve their goals.

Meaningless segmentation

There is one gap where the problem is not lack of application but one of widespread practice; one that is not just wrong but could be damaging. This is the categorisation of customers as "high touch", "medium touch" or "tech touch" customers.[9] Mea culpa: it is an error I have made in the past.

The Business Dictionary defines segmentation as *"the process of defining and subdividing a large homogenous market into clearly identifiable segments having similar needs, wants, or demand characteristics"*.[10] Put simply, segmentation should identify a group of people that will respond positively to the same action.

[9] The definition of high, medium and tech touch describes the level of service offered and one of the ten laws cited in *Customer Success* (ibid)

[10] http://www.businessdictionary.com/definition/market-segmentation.html

High/medium/tech touch fails on both counts: their spend does not indicate similar needs, and it fails to suggest actions that everyone in that so-called segment will respond to positively.

Unfortunately, this simplistic approach, based on how much customers spend with you, is used by many companies to decide on the level of intervention that customers receive. It confuses segmentation with affordability and results in your customers receiving a form of service that has no meaningful basis to what is needed to ensure their success and, thereby, the renewal and growth of their subscription. The idea that every one of your customers is one of three types, determined by spend, is the antithesis of customer centricity. But as the 17th century French diplomat De Tocqueville said, "*It is easier for the world to accept a simple lie than a complex truth.*" In Chapter Nine, I will suggest an approach that does away with the need for segmentation as it is currently practiced in many B2B SaaS companies.

CS as a company-wide commitment

This is probably the biggest gap of all and the one that led me to write this book. The challenge and solution to CS as a company-wide capability lies at your door.

In his excellent book *Subscribed*[11], Tien Tzuou, CEO of Zuora, perfectly describes how most CEOs address new challenges: "*When in doubt, build another vertical silo.*" This, unfortunately, is how most companies address the challenge of delivering value to customers. Whilst the need for a customer success team is clear, it alone cannot address the product, processes and metrics needed across the company to deliver meaningful customer success. That is an organisation design challenge; to purposefully design your organisation to "profitably win, satisfy, retain and grow its chosen customers better than the competition". Companies often fail to fulfil their potential because you, the CEO, fail

────────────────────────────

[11] Subscribed: Why the Subscription Model Will Be Your Company's Future - and What to Do About It. Tien Tzuo. ISBN 978-0-241-36366-9

in your primary task of chief organisation design officer. Creating a department, charging it with delivering customer success and demanding alignment with other departments is fundamentally different from designing to consistently deliver value to customers.

CS vs CS vs CS vs CX

Few things are more pointless than the endless articles and associated discussions about which version of customer focus is more important; is it customer success, customer service, customer support, customer experience. As soon as one article explains that customer success is a subset of customer experience, another appears arguing the exact opposite with the same passion. There are many variants of this: customer success is more than customer support; customer journeys are part of the customer experience discipline; CSMs and account managers are different things, and one is more important. Pick any pair and construct your argument.

It is easy to spot the stance an individual will take on this: look at their job title or business. It is a classic case of confirmation bias: hammers tend to see nails; screwdrivers, screws.

I have a simple take on this: call it Freda! The overwhelming majority of customers don't care what you call it, so why should you? I don't. OK, that may be a bit glib, but the underlying point is important. Our understanding of what it takes to build true customer focus has developed over time, and new ideas, technology and experience will enable new ways of understanding and delivering what customers want. Change is a constant. Your job as CEO is to take the best of the new ideas and approaches that are relevant to your customers and your business and weave them into your organisation. Over 40 years, I have used different labels and adopted new ideas but kept to the same overarching principle: "Customer [insert your own label] is everything an organisation does to profitably win, satisfy, retain and grow its chosen customers better than the competition." I now use the term customer success simply because that resonates with my chosen customers – B2B SaaS companies and their investors. I predict that in a few years a new label will come along and everyone will jump on it.

All the gaps described above are manifestations of the same thing a company that is fad surfing and not truly focused on its customers. Building a company-wide commitment to customers is an organisation design challenge. It requires you, the CEO, to understand the broader implications of customer success and, more importantly, purposefully design your organisation to deliver it. That is the focus of this book.

2: New challenges: new approaches

The gaps described in the previous chapter have been around for several years but are compounded by more recent developments. Here are the challenges and approaches I think are shaping B2B SaaS businesses.

Spiralling acquisition costs

The growth and acceptance of SaaS as a business model has seen an explosion in the number of companies adopting it. New companies appear daily, and old-style software companies are busily transforming their value propositions, products and organisations to become SaaS providers. One problem this has created is the cost of acquiring new customers.

Anyone selling SaaS in its first decade will be familiar with this scenario. Marketing created awareness through content, events, search and cold-calling, generating leads which, at a certain point, were passed to sales. Sales, hopefully after researching the company, began a conversation with a contact, which led to multiple other contacts. A demonstration was set up, which if successful created the opportunity to negotiate and hopefully close a deal. Research from CEB[12] suggests that, on average, 5.4 people are involved in a decision to purchase a SaaS software product; 6 to 11 for complex products! More content is needed for more people involved in the buying decision, further increasing costs. Dealing with this number of buyers requires more marketing and sales effort, extending the sale cycle and increasing acquisition costs.

As more suppliers enter the market, often addressing narrow niches, more companies are bidding for search keywords, pushing up the price. Content marketers are becoming more expensive as the volume of content pushed out by B2B companies expands significantly. Target buyers are swamped by the explosion of content, which is also driving

[12] https://www.challengerinc.com/sales

down the number of shares. Now, only great content that addresses the specific needs of target customers has any chance of meaningful success and that is fleeting. Growth itself increases costs. Early customers recognise readily the pain point the company is addressing and are willing to be early adopters. Once this low hanging fruit is captured, more effort is needed to build awareness and drive conversion.

The upshot, according to SaaS data specialists Profitwell, is a 50% increase in the cost of acquisition (CAC) of B2B customers over the last five years.[13] Generating the best possible return on increasing CAC places greater importance on retaining and growing those expensively acquired customers.

Freemium and atomisation of the buyer

This high-cost acquisition model is still very commonplace and, in some circumstances – notably applications that have to be implemented enterprise-wide, may be a valid approach. There is, however, a fundamental change underway. Software acquisition is driven increasingly by individuals and teams, not entire companies. Faced with a specific need, many users will find and adopt software of their choosing, taking advantage of free or very low-cost offerings. They don't have the time nor inclination to convince their company to buy a new software package. They don't know how to navigate a selection and procurement process. They just want to get on and do their job. Conditioned by the instant availability of applications on ecosystems like Apple's Appstore or Google's Workspace Marketplace, users now expect instant access and a richly-featured free app or free trial. This is another example of the consumerisation of business software.

These individual buyers rarely want to get involved with a salesperson. Equally, the companies supplying software in this way can't afford a

---

[13] https://www.profitwell.com/blog/content-marketing-customer-acquisition-cost

traditional sales motion and even if they could, few traditional salespeople would be interested in the volumes and low commission potential of low average sales values. What these buyers want is a product they can access immediately, use immediately and get value from immediately. This changes the customer lifecycle fundamentally.

The traditional SaaS model of engagement can be characterised as:

> See -> Try -> Buy -> Use -> Value

Atomisation of the buyer, enabled by the freemium business model, rearranges the steps:

> See-> Value -> Buy -> Value -> [Buy -> Value]^n

This cycle also starts with marketing driving traffic, increasingly using viral techniques, but changes thereafter. The fundamental shift is that customers expect to see value, to experience the magic if, or even **before,** they buy. Conversion to a paying customer begins the value cycle again, but payment often raises expectations so delivering value repeatedly is essential to secure renewals and expansion.

With the product-led model, revenue is generated by customers that buy, not by salespeople selling. Delivering value (aka customer success) becomes the central driver of the initial and subsequent sales motions. The linear representation of the funnel, even the dicky-bow, are redundant. Modern B2B SaaS is a repeating cycle of value-enabled buying, where the maxim for the supplier is "deliver or die".

Software disrupts everything

Success as software

If the purpose of your B2B SaaS company is to help someone achieve their goal, then this should be the purpose and focus of your product. As discussed above, achieving success often requires more than adopting software. This is why SaaS companies invest in customer success but despite "Product is your only sustainable differentiator" being one of the ten laws in Customer Success (ibid), few SaaS products have a value-driven success process built in. I first proposed this approach to the CEO of a UK-based SaaS company in 2015 and then went on to develop the idea further, publishing the idea in an e-book in 2016. The idea was dismissed by many, including that CEO. Detractors argued that delivering customer success was too complex and required human intervention. This ignores significant developments and thinking that are shaping the world of software. It also ignores an increasing number of startups that are building their products around a success process. Oh, and by the way, the naysayers' products are "too complex" because their companies have built them that way.

User interface

It is a rare beast that does not play video games. Whether a casual gamer playing Solitaire on the train to work or a seasoned master playing the latest version of a highly complex role-playing game, gaming is ubiquitous. Game developers know that success requires mastery of usability, flow, and look and feel. They know the importance of getting players playing quickly, of setting challenges and guiding players through the story. These are the same type of challenges facing your company when dealing with customers, but you call it onboarding, advice and guidance, and value achievement.

Game developers set the standard that your business software has to meet for usability and motivation. To win in today's business application marketplace, your software has to look stunning and be ridiculously easy to use, whatever the user's level of expertise. The know-how exists, but few B2B SaaS companies employ it.

Psychology and software

One thing both gaming and social media developers understand and employ is psychology. Fear of missing out and the dopamine fix are employed to keep us checking social media feeds with their endless scroll. Game developers employ reward and learning theories to motivate players to ever new levels of attainment. Whilst some of these techniques are misused and (rightly) viewed as harmful, understanding and applying psychology to driving in-app value delivery processes provides huge promise.

Machine learning and artificial intelligence

Delivering customer success is most effective when different datasets are brought together to inform the customer's current context as the basis for deciding the next steps. Layering machine learning (ML) onto a rich dataset allows companies to identify and act on patterns of activity that drive customer success. Expect to see these powerful technologies play an increasing role in uncovering the activities that drive value.

One of the most interesting concepts that builds on ML/AI is "anti-active-usage software".[14] Most of today's software requires people to drive both systems of record (data-oriented systems like CRM) and workflow systems. As ML/AI become more sophisticated, systems will take on much of the work of interpreting the data and deciding and implementing the action to be taken. This fundamentally changes the nature of customer success.

Rethinking customer success

These changes in the way SaaS software is built, bought and used have massive implications for B2B SaaS companies and how you should think about and deliver value to customers.

Person not company

The premise is that a company buys business software to address a challenge or an opportunity, so the outcome has to deliver a measurable benefit to the company. Success plans are developed that focus on the company's desired outcome. The underlying assumption

---

[14] The Next Generation of SaaS Won't Optimize for User Engagement. https://leonardofed.io/blog/saas.html

is that different roles are team players in a game with the same goal. The company is the determinant of value.

This premise is wrong on two counts. Atomisation of the buyer has changed the buying unit for many B2B applications. Understanding the needs, expectations and work of the individual is, therefore, the key to both the initial sale and retention/expansion. Even in sales of enterprise software, success at all stages of the customer lifecycle is dependent on understanding, shaping and achievement of goals of different individuals.

The shift to focus on individuals and the use of psychology is explored in Chapter Six: "People not customers".

Minutes and hours not months and years

In the 1990s, a multi-national customer of mine decided to implement a new ERP system. The project involved hundreds of members of staff, contractors and consultants (not me) and took almost five years to implement. Such was the challenge of getting users to adopt this behemoth that at one point the team gave users project swag – mugs saying: "Resistance is futile".

Fast forward 25 years. Download an app from the AppStore and it is available instantly and, in the vast majority of cases, you will be using it in minutes: all without the intervention of a salesperson, an implementation team or a customer success manager. Of course, there is a difference in scale but that is the expectation of software apps today.

The howls of sceptics saying that's OK for games, consumer or simple apps are deafening. In most cases, they are wrong. Individuals increasingly want to get started immediately and see value quickly. Their timescales for implementing, using and seeing value are measured in hours and days, not months and years.

Value Elements not outcomes

Companies that have implemented customer success plans have focused on the outcome the company seeks. When asked, most describe it as a high-level, measurable (preferably financial) business goal. Achieving this outcome or goal is rarely achieved by mastery of the product alone: it almost always involves some changes to working practices, skills and metrics.

As expectations of time-to-value shrink and the focus on the individual grows, this singular goal becomes problematic, even in enterprise software implementation. A singular goal is often distant from the people using the application and requires the involvement of people and processes beyond the core users. In his excellent article,[15] Rav Dhaliwal talked of "buyers vs deployers" and the importance of "understanding the 'distance' between the purchaser and the deployer/end user".

Like beauty, value is in the eye of the beholder: taking a more granular approach to value is therefore needed.

Digital, not people, first

Fifteen years ago, setting up a CS capability was all about hiring a team of CSMs to deliver the customer success capability. Today, many companies begin with a digital first approach, where the basic value delivery process is automated. This has numerous advantages:

- It meets the increasing preference of customers for a self-serve approach as a first step;
- It allows an affordable, success process to be delivered to all customers;

---

[15] "There's no such thing as post-sale"
https://medium.com/@ravsterd/theres-no-such-thing-as-post-sales-a2dd1bfb3efc

- It removes people from basic, repetitive tasks, freeing them up to do higher value, more engaging work;
- Digital first enables scale at profit, contributing to improved valuations.

Let's be very clear, digital first does not mean digital only! Nor does a digital first approach mean the end of a separate CS team and CSMs. Digital first frees up time to take on higher order, more challenging tasks to which people are uniquely suited.

Organisation by design, not alignment

One of the biggest failings I have seen B2B SaaS companies make is buying churn. Driven by a misplaced understanding of growth, they seek to attract customers irrespective of their ability to deliver the meaningful value that underpins reliable retention and growth. This, however, is just one example of an affliction facing many companies: the lack of alignment across departments and teams.

I have come to the conclusion that the quest for alignment is, fundamentally, the failure of the CEO and leadership team to purposefully design a customer-focused organisation. It is a problem that is ineffectively resolved by what I call retro-alignment: an attempt to bridge gaps that result from leaving individual departments to define their processes and metrics in isolation. They all try to do their best for the customer but all take a narrow approach focused on their profession.

In Chapter Five - "Success by design", I will explain why success for customers is the basis for purposeful organisation design and how you can achieve it.

Remember your roots

You started a B2B SaaS company because you found a new or better way to use software, a product, to solve a problem. You may well have worked in that domain, experienced that challenge and been dissatisfied with the solutions available. You understand the issues and know what a successful solution looks like and, importantly, how its value is measured. You know that lots of other people face the same problem, so you can define and size a target market. In essence, a new SaaS business is founded on understanding and delivering customer success.

This knowledge and experience is the basis you used to build out a value proposition. "What problem do you solve for who?" and "How is your product a better answer than others?" are questions every CEO must answer to attract customers and funding. You'll find answers to these questions in every successful funding pitch deck. B2B investors want to know that your business addresses a real need in a measurable way to a sufficiently large addressable market. Customer success – the capability, not just the team – is how you address that.

Much has changed in the 15 years since I appointed my first CSM. There have been real improvements in the recognition of the importance of customer success and how it is practiced. Unfortunately, many companies have yet to recognise the underlying changes, and as a result they are failing to adapt how they practice customer success. They argue that their business is different (it is and always has been), that their product is too complex (their fault) and that customers are too demanding to want anything other than a high touch, people-based service (they often prefer self-service).

I think the best companies keep the founder's belief at the heart of what they do as they grow and bring everyone and everything back to the customer. Growth understandably brings the need for specialisation and that, without great care and effort, brings fragmentation. Remember the words of Tien Tzuo: "*When in doubt, build another vertical silo.*" In my experience, this has the discipline of customer success writ large. I hope that after reading this book, you will be better equipped as a CEO.

3: The fundamentals

Before we get into the weeds, I want to set out the basis of my thinking, which underpins the approach I advocate.

Company-wide customer success

To me, company-wide customer success capability is

> *"Everything an organisation does*
>
> *to profitably*
>
> *win, satisfy, retain and grow*
>
> *its chosen customers*
>
> *better than the competition."*

I do not apologise for repeating this definition; it is fundamental to your challenge of building a successful B2B SaaS business. It has guided much of what will follow, so I want to break it down into its constituent parts because every line, every word matters.

Everything an organisation does. This highlights the most fundamental characteristic of customer success: it's not about what a team called customer success does. Customer success defines your value proposition, the customer acquisition process, post sales operations and, of course, the product itself. It shapes what people pay attention to, reinforced by leaders that understand the broader concept of customer success. It is why you, the CEO, has to take responsibility for purposefully building alignment into the organisation, not leaving it to be retro-fitted.

to profitably. This may not apply to the early stages of your growth, but at some point investors and markets will want to see the company achieve profitability or show a path to achieving it. Customer success is easy to achieve, but profitable customer success requires more considered thought and sustained execution. Understanding the financial elements of customer success, its revenue contribution, productivity and impact on enterprise value is essential to growing business the right way.

win, satisfy, retain and grow. Customer success is at the core of every step taken with the customer. This also reinforces the "everything" perspective and, for me, explains why companies that view CS as what a post-sale team does are doomed to under-perform. This also points to the importance of a joined-up journey.

its chosen customers. Most B2B value propositions only work for customers that share certain characteristics. Focusing on these and building a deep understanding of their needs and how your company delivers value is key. I have seen too many cases where especially growth stage companies kill their unit economics by chasing any customer only to discover they cannot meet their needs and lose them to churn early in their life.

better than the competition. Doing all the above will come to naught if a competitor does it better. Whilst most will think about direct competitors who offer a similar product, many businesses lose to a different type of competitor: the battle for the customer's mind-space. New-logo sales and renewals often fail not to competitor products but because the customer has other priorities or believes the risks outweigh the gains. It is why an intense focus on the value achieved by your chosen customers is critical.

It is clear to me that many of the mistakes and inefficiencies facing some (many?) B2B SaaS companies stem from the failure to understand fully this broader concept of customer success. Many of those that do understand it often fail to drive the company-wide execution it needs.

How I think about organisations

Many of the problems we face in delivering a company-wide approach to customer success have their roots in how we think about organisations; specifically the paradigms on which our thinking is based.

Organisation and management theory is rooted in mechanistic models: hierarchies, cause and effect chains, logic and rationale. This goes back to the industrial revolution, when employment shifted from agriculture to factories in a time when the class system was even more deeply rooted than today. Starting with Adam Smith's ideas on specialisation of labour, early management thinkers like Taylor, Fayol and the Gilbreths used mechanical metaphors as the basis of their thinking. Organisations were encouraged to impose hierarchies, chains of command and detailed measurement.

The ideas of scientific management still dominate much of our thinking today. We are advised to build our organisations around the specialist departments, to create hierarchies of people and ideas and establish performance-based pay that focuses on the individual. The mechanistic or reductionist approach tells us that a single outcome can be broken down into its constituent parts, and clearly defined inputs and tightly controlled processes will consistently deliver the same output. This hierarchical approach mirrors the organisation charts we love so much. The problem is that organisations, yours and your customers', are not mechanistic – because people aren't.

There are areas of science and nature that suggest other approaches. Which termite organises its peers to build and maintain the massive, complex structures they inhabit? Which fish is the leader of a shoal that instructs others to change direction? Who tells a bee where to go and look for food? The concepts of hierarchy and the single leader directing everything are absent in all of them. Physics even provides seemingly contradictory views to the seemingly predictable nature of the world around us. Newtonian laws describe a predictable universe, where events far in the future are known. Quantum mechanics, however, tells us that what we measure determines what we see; that particles separated by huge distances seem to maintain an unknown relationship and that much of what makes up our world and the universe is not visible and, as of today, can't be seen or measured. And yet, the quantum and Newtonian (deterministic) worlds co-exist. Even mathematics, the most "rational" of our sciences, sparks new metaphors. The beauty of many of nature's features, from coastlines to ferns, are fractal phenomena.

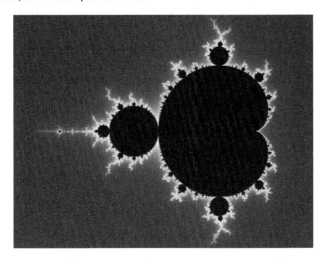

Fig 3.1 Example of a fractal image

Fractal equations are relatively simple but include feedback loops that reflect what is happening at the edge. Despite this simplicity, they produce some of the most beautiful patterns: patterns that cannot be predicted but have a simple, repeating theme at their core. For me, visions and values are an organisation's fractal equation, enabling independence of action and fostering creativity whilst maintaining elegant coherence.

Thinking about people has also developed. For years, motivation specialists told us that whilst the absence of sufficient money is a de-motivator, above a certain level, more money is not an effective motivator: that intrinsic factors like freedom of choice, shared purpose, continuous learning and relationships are more effective. Yet pay-for-individual performance still dominates the practice of organisation rewards. Psychologists have learned massively about how we think and the in-built, often hard-wired, thinking patterns that fool us.

Whilst there are exceptions, management theory is still dogged by legacy thinking; an unwillingness or inability to rethink the way we build and enable organisations and the people they employ. Scientific management, designed in the early days of manufacturing and reflecting the science of the time, has failed to keep up with science. There are many examples of organisations adopting more naturalistic approaches to organisation design and managing people. For those wanting to explore this important field in greater depth (and I encourage you to), study the examples of companies like Haier, Semco or Happy Computers. Corporate Rebels[16] is a great starting point for case studies and advice.

Not all the ideas in scientific management are wrong, and the answer lies in blending the best of the old and the new, but I make no apologies that many of the practices in this book are inspired by "the new sciences". As George Bernard Shaw said, "*The reasonable man adapts himself to the world: the unreasonable one persists in trying to adapt the world to himself. Therefore, all progress depends on the unreasonable man.*" I want a world where we focus on people, not faceless customers. A world where continuous incremental value replaces the failed attempts to impose big-bang, top-down outcomes. A world where automation replaces drudgery at work, leaving people to do more challenging, engaging work.

My natural tendency is always to ask two questions. The first is "*Why do we do that at all?*" If the resulting debate and data provide a valid reason, then the second question is "*Why do we do it that way?*" This desire to be the rebel, the heretic, is what has led me to the seven principles that underpin customer-led growth that I will set out in Part Two. They are shaped by own experience as both an employee and an entrepreneur. In the spirit of George Bernard Shaw, they are shaped by being proudly and loudly unreasonable.

---

[16] www.corporate-rebels.com

PART TWO

The seven principles of customer success

This part of the book explains the seven principles needed to craft a company-wide customer success capability. Here's where you'll find the main ideas.

4: Principle One – Customer success is a financial strategy

I contend that in B2B SaaS, customer success is the core of your business; it is how your company makes money. It is important, therefore, that you understand its financial contribution.

Customer success drives valuations

My interest in building customer success capabilities is founded on hard-headed finance. Valuing a company is part science and part gut-feel; the answer differs, therefore, by gut-owner. I have been through the process from both sides. I sold my SaaS company twice and have been involved in the due-diligence process with investors. Whilst I am not an expert, I have learned that valuations are shaped by a number of factors, key of which are:

- Size and type of revenue: Scale of, recurring or one-off, product or services;
- Growth rate;
- Business model: How the company acquires and services its customers;
- Predictability: How sure the company is of future revenues;
- Total Addressable Market: How big is the market the company can acquire;
- Productivity: How efficiently the company uses its cash;
- Profitability: What margin the company makes or has the potential to make;
- Unit economics: What is cost and return of the key drivers of revenue and operations;
- Free cash flow: How the company generates and consumes cash;
- Sentiment: What investors feel about the leadership team, the market and the product;

- The market: Investors have a herd mentality, so value is shaped by the collective view of the market.

Customer success capability influences many of these factors.

The most significant impact is the revenue generated from existing customers. In a well-run SaaS business, renewals and expansion revenue quickly become the biggest source of revenue. For example, a company growing new business sales at 100% with Net Revenue Retention of 105% will see revenue from existing customers exceed new business sales in four years. Whilst I am not saying it is easy, I believe that sustaining NRR above 100% is less challenging than sustaining new business growth of 20% in the long term.

It is clear, therefore, that retention and expansion of existing customers is equally as important as new business acquisition, although you would not assume that if you look at the time most CEOs spend on the two. I believe this is a vestige of the "win and move on" thinking that dominated the old technology sales model, where revenue was front loaded and not dependent on continued subscriptions. If you think of your customer success capability as something you only need after you have won your first customers, you are making the mistake of thinking of customer success as a discrete team and not a fundamental, company-wide capability. Investor Rav Dhaliwal puts it eloquently: *"there is no such thing as post-sales but rather there is the first sale with a customer, the next sale with them and so on, and in order to maximise the conditions for this, Customer Success has to begin in the sales-cycle."* [ibid].

A focus on customer success has other effects that help improve the company's enterprise value. The costs associated with retaining and growing revenue from existing customers is significantly less than new logo acquisition. Data from the widely respected "For Entrepreneurs" annual survey of private SaaS companies reports the following Customer Acquisition Costs (CAC)[17]:

---

[17] For Entrepreneurs 2017 Private SaaS Survey. More recent surveys show a similar pattern but have not separately reported

- New business $1.34;
- Upsell $0.57;
- Expansion sales $0.30;
- Renewal $0.15.

Think about that: every $ you invest in securing a renewal generates a nine-fold greater return than the same $ invested in acquiring new customers. It explains the importance of addressing the leaky barrel; for a small additional investment, expensively won customers can be turned into a predictable, long term revenue source. Of course, you cannot retain and grow a customer you didn't win in the first place, so I am not suggesting companies don't spend on it. Together, the growth contribution and lower costs of acquisition of revenue from existing customers makes a significant contributor to your profitability; another of the drivers of enterprise valuations.

Customers that achieve their goals with your product also generate positive word of mouth and thereby help attract new customers. This may be from direct referrals, acting as references, providing case studies or just extolling your value to friends and colleagues. This secondary source of revenue is invaluable for several reasons. When sales leaders in 400 companies were asked about referrals[18]:

- 82% said they are the best leads you can get;
- 75% said they have a higher conversion rate;
- 70% said they convert quicker;
- 59% said they have a higher LTV.

Whilst B2B research is thin on the ground, quantitative research into the financial impact of advocacy in B2C shows that compared to leads from other sources, advocacy-based leads:

---

cost of renewal. The figures reported are the cost of acquiring $1 of revenue.

[18] https://influitive.com/infographic-17-stats-about-b2b-referrals-you-should-know-but-probably-dont/

- Have 37% higher retention than leads from other sources;[19]
- Generate between 16% to 25% higher LTV;[20]
- Return a 25% higher profit margin;
- Convert from leads to business at the rate of other leads.

The power of advocacy to generate revenue with a lower cost of acquisition is dependent on customer success. A customer is highly unlikely to recommend or endorse your company unless they have achieved the value they expected and have trust in your company. Remember, when someone recommends you, they are putting their reputation, not just yours, on the line.

An important factor in SaaS company valuations is predictability of revenue. Investors love companies which can give high levels of certainty around future revenues. SaaS generally fits the bill and revenue from existing customers forms a big part of this. Your renewal number is known in advance; it's predictable if the process of delivering customers value is effective. Couple this with the increasing share of revenue from existing customers and you have CS contributing significantly to predictable revenue, thus enhancing your company's valuation.

Along with the LTV:CAC ratio, NRR is one of the most important indicators of the health of a B2B SaaS business. Why? Because it correlates with enterprise valuations, as the chart below shows.[21]

---

[19] https://www.slideshare.net/brandonmurphy/brand-advocacy-and-social-media-2009-gma-conference/11-Are_you_activating_your_advocatesConsumers

[20] https://knowledge.wharton.upenn.edu/article/turning-social-capital-into-economic-capital-straight-talk-about-word-of-mouth-marketing/

[21] Zoom is an outlier partly because this data dates from the height of the COVID pandemic. That said, Zoom also benefits from high NRR.

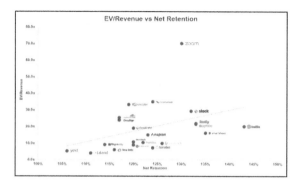

Fig 4.1: NRR and enterprise value[22]

Just think about the major metrics that investors and markets follow and how they are impacted by your customer success capability.

- NRR increases through increased renewals and improved expansion sales;
- CAC is reduced;
- LTV is increased as churn falls;
- NPS is improved as customers value what you deliver;
- Productivity improves as duplication and internal friction reduces;
- Funding costs are cut as lower churn reduces burn rate;
- Valuation improves as growth accelerates!

CS and business models

In Chapter Two, I discussed some of the changes that are shaping B2B SaaS businesses. SaaS leaders have to understand these changes and how they affect operations.

---

[22] Source: Software Equity Group. The Impact of Net Retention on Valuation for Public SaaS Companies. 30 July 2020.

	On-premise	SaaS V1	SaaS V2
EXEMPLARS	Oracle, IBM, SAP	Salesforce, Workday	Slack, Atlassian
VALUE FOCUS	Brand Reputation	Features & outcomes	Value elements
BUYER	Corporate IT	Department/BU	Individual/team
MARKETING FOCUS	Brand	Content	Viral product
CUSTOMER ACQUISITION	Field sales	Inside sales	Product-led
PRICING MODEL	Eternal license	Subscription	Consumption/Value
PRODUCT FOCUS	Features	Configurable	Ease of use & Value
TIME TO VALUE	Months/Years	Weeks/Months	Hours/Days
KEY METRICS	Sales bookings	ARR, CAC, Churn	LTV, Conversion, NRR
KEY CAPABILITY	Selling	Retention	Expansion
VALUATION MULTIPLE	Low	Average	High

Fig 4.2: Evolution of software business models

This chart summarises the main changes I see happening as software business models evolve. It is important to recognise that the three columns are not discrete; companies will often operate with elements of more than one business model. Nor does it imply that companies operating the more traditional business models will fail. Most models can deliver success if well executed. I do believe though that, just as SaaS V1 became the primary software business model, SaaS V2 will come to dominate, driven by the twin engines of customer preference and financial return.

SaaS drove the shift to the subscription business model in the software industry with one-time, perpetual licence sales replaced by recurring revenue. This not only changed the shape of the revenue profile, but it also shifted the risk to the supplier, requiring them to actively contribute to the success the customer required to justify continued subscription payments. The investment and growth model for the first wave of SaaS was established: invest in acquisition and retention to drive growth and secure a growing and often dominant market share.

The second wave of SaaS draws on the experience of the B2C software market. Consumers supposedly lack the sophistication of businesses, requiring software that looks nice and is ridiculously easy to use. Mass markets make the support model commonplace in B2B software unaffordable, which drives investment in in-product capabilities. Understanding what drives the needs of individuals is the key to adoption, and a viral element keeps adoption high and reduces the cost of acquisition. Of course, many consumers are exactly the same people that have work-related needs. It is obvious, therefore, that what works in a consumer context can be applied, with some adjustment, to a business context. The atomisation of the buyer and the commensurate focus on rapid, repeatable Value Elements looks more like a B2C model.

The shift from on-premise to SaaS V1 changed revenue profiles but also the cost structure of the P&L. The move to SaaS V2 changes this profile again. Consider the following data from publicly listed SaaS companies.

	SALESFORCE	ADOBE	SERVICENOW	DATADOG	ATLASSIAN
Cost of revenues (GP)	25%	15%	23%	25%	17%
Research & Development	16%	17%	22%	31%	48%
Marketing & Sales	46%	29%	44%	40%	22%
General & Administration	10%	8%	10%	10%	18%
Annualised revenue value multiple	6.1x	12.2x	14.2x	20.7x	18.2x

Fig 4.3: Cost breakdown (as %age of revenue) for selected public SaaS companies

Whilst there are no hard and fast rules, product-led companies like DataDog and Atlassian spend proportionately more on research and development and less on marketing and sales compared with companies founded early in the SaaS lifetime. This reflects the way they sell to and service their customers, with a greater proportion of the work being delivered through the product. CS costs typically form part of marketing and sales, so a smaller proportion of the revenue is available to fund CS activities. How CS capability is delivered has to adapt to and reflect the business model: the traditional approach is not sustainable. The SaaS V1 approach of building out a team of CSMs gives way to building a digital first capability. In my mind, that suggests a fundamentally different approach to building CS capability, including the hiring pattern, processes, metrics and organisational model.

Monetising customer success

There is another way that customer success contributes to both customer and company success: charging for services that help the customer achieve their goals. In this context, that includes any fee-paying offering. Some companies use the term professional services to describe these fee-paying services and thus distinguish them from free customer success services.

Charging for customer success is a topic I researched in late 2019. Here are the highlights:

- 70% of respondents are either offering or planning to introduce fee paying customer success services;
- Monetising CS presents significant growth opportunities with 30% of respondents generating between 2% and 5% of revenues from such services, whilst 16% say services contributes over 20% to revenues;
- The contribution of services is significantly lower than that of product revenues. Only 34% of respondents reported services gross margins of 20% or higher. SaaS product gross margins typically exceed 70%. It is this that causes many investors to question SaaS companies with a high ratio of services revenue;
- The practice is not just the domain of SaaS companies selling to enterprise customers: companies serving all types of B2B customers are charging for some services;
- Sales lead the way in selling CS services with 90% responsible for services sales to new businesses and 41% to existing customers. CS takes the lead in selling services to existing customers in 43% of respondents;
- Fears over a negative impact on retention was the most quoted reason for not charging for services, but only 2% of respondents that do charge say it has a negative impact. 39% report a positive impact on retention with a further 21% saying it had no impact.

This last point is crucial: fee paying services often improve retention, which is customer success' biggest revenue contributor. HubSpot, (a case study in the research) which offers a range of fee-paying success services, say that customers buying services use their products five times more than other customers and are 20% more likely to renew.

The reticence to charge is often a philosophical objection. One respondent to the survey said, *"Charging contradicts the CS concept."* This reflects a broader point of view held by many that helping customers and selling to them are incompatible. Those that do not support charging for customer success services fail to recognise a number of points:

- Many customers recognise that value is rarely achieved by technology alone and look to the supplier to provide some of the expertise and leg work required. They understand the value of this and expect to pay;
- Implementing new technologies often causes a peak in workloads in the early stages. It is often easier and cheaper for the customer to buy in the additional resources to do this. This is especially true when the supplier brings the expertise and experience gained by working with many other customers. Even ongoing services can be cheaper than hiring in-house resources;
- When budgeting for new technologies, especially enterprise implementations, customers often include services in their budgets;
- Paid for services allow SaaS suppliers to provide capabilities that can shorten the time needed for a customer to achieve value or provide access to higher levels of value.

The research and my own experience lead me to believe that selling services is the right thing to do, but ground rules have to be established.

- Just like the product, services need to be built around the delivery of specific value;
- Any required (mandatory) services are explained early in the sales process, setting out clearly the price, scope and benefits of what is required;
- Service propositions make clear what effort and resources the customer has to commit to complete the service;
- The characteristics of customers that can benefit from specific services are clearly identified and used to qualify opportunities;

- Clear measures are established for value achieved and time to value.

A focus on customers and the value they seek is at the core of the financial success of your SaaS business. The rest of this book explores the foundational role customer success capability plays; how it is the core of your product and value proposition, the basis of the acquisition process and the focus of post-sale activity. This red thread connecting the spine of the company's value chain is a powerful mechanism for driving growth, productivity, profitability and, therefore, enterprise value.

5: Principle Two – Success by design

"All organisations are perfectly designed to get the results they get."

I love this quote by Arthur Jones. It sums up the essence of the challenge many CEOs face. It is a challenge few have mastered. If you want proof of that, just look at the plethora of articles about aligning [*insert name of a department*] and [*insert name of any other department*].

Many of these articles proffer similar advice: master your handoffs, share data and foster collaboration; one article suggested salespeople should buy a CSM a beer or a coffee. Some get closer to the heart of the issue and implore companies to develop a common customer understanding, share content and build personas. The common thread and root of the problem is that alignment is retro-fitted, an attempt to paste over flaws inherent in silo-based thinking. As CEO, you are responsible for the design of your organisation. The first principle of building a truly customer-focused B2B SaaS business is purposeful organisation design.

> *"Today, the only way to ensure success is to reorient everything your business does around the customer. Make sure that all departments of the organisation, and all staff, clearly understand that what they do and how they do it affects customers, and therefore the organisation's ability to deliver on its promises."*
>
> **Gero Decker, Co-founder & CEO,** Signavio[23]

---

[23] https://www.eu-startups.com/2020/03/your-continued-growth-as-an-organisation-relies-on-staying-hungry-interview-with-signavios-founder-gero/

An architect's guide to organisation design

Architects can teach us a lesson in organisation design. In 1896, American architect Louis Sullivan said "*It is the pervading law of all things organic and inorganic, of all things physical and metaphysical, of all things human and all things superhuman, of all true manifestations of the head, of the heart, of the soul, that the life is recognizable in its expression, that form ever follows function. This is the law.*" [24] In shorthand, **form follows function.** Before putting pencil to paper, a good architect seeks to build a deep understanding of the purpose of the building, the characteristics and needs of the people who will use it and how they will assess the suitability of the building. What spaces will different users need? What services will they require? How many people will the building serve, and how will different users move through and around the building, doing what? What environment is needed? Only then will the architect begin to develop the overall look and feel of the building. As this evolves, specialists like structural engineers, electricians and plumbers add details of the different services needed to make the building function but all within the framework of the architect's overall design thesis.

"Form follows function" teaches us that how an organisation is structured should be driven by its purpose and its work. This means figuring out why the organisation exists, who it serves and how it functions before worrying about structure. So many mistakes are made and problems created because we do the opposite. We focus on the lines and boxes, roles and responsibilities before figuring out purpose and process. This focus on structure also misses the point that much of what makes the organisation successful is how the different parts work together; the informal processes of communication, collaboration and innovation. These vital elements never appear in an organisation chart.

─────────────────────────────

[24] Louis H, Sullivan, "The Tall Office Building Artistically Considered". Lippincott's Magazine (March 1896)

Designing a customer-centric business

You need to purposefully design your organisation to deliver value to your chosen customers. This requires five things:

- A shared understanding of the **purpose and values of the organisation** – why your "building" exists and what fundamental principles guide how things get done. For B2B SaaS, I contend that purpose centres around the value you deliver to your chosen customers;
- Clarity and company-wide agreement on the **characteristics of your chosen customers**;
- A high-level, outside-in design of **how you engage your chosen customers** across the complete acquisition and use lifecycle;
- Agreement on a small number of **measures that apply to everyone**;
- The **soft processes** the organisation uses to foster collaboration, innovation and alignment in pursuit of purpose and values.

Let's take each of these five elements and their role in building an organisation focused on delivering value to customers.

Shared purpose and values

Purpose[25] and values are the bedrock of organisation design: they create a framework in which bottom-up contributions are harnessed to a broad direction.

Here's a few examples of purpose statements:

- **Clicktools**: Help our chosen customers better understand and serve their customers

---

[25] I use the word purpose. Others may refer to this as vision or mission. The common factor is that it answers the question "Why do we exist?"

- **Google**: Organize the world's information and make it universally accessible and useful
- **LinkedIn**: Create economic opportunity for every member of the global workforce
- **Tesla**: Accelerate the world's transition to sustainable energy
- **TED**: Spread ideas

Each of these provide a high-level answer to the question "Why do we exist?" but say nothing about how that purpose will be fulfilled. Note the heading says shared purpose, which means it is understood by people across the organisation. The words are a catalyst to drive conversations which build shared understanding, which in turn shape decisions, collaboration and action. It may be axiomatic, but the more that purpose and values are challenged and debated, the stronger they become. There is much more than a semantic difference between a shared purpose and a purpose shared.

Purpose provides an innate, deep-felt need most people have to understand their role and contribution without being proscriptive about how. "*Purpose affirms trust, trust affirms purpose, and together they forge individuals into a working team.*" [26] Those are the words of the US Army's General Stanley McChrystal. He adds "*Order emerges from the bottom up and shouldn't be directed from the top down.*" What the US Army has learned recently, nature has known for millennia. Termites, bees, mackerel and so many other species succeed because they interact as independent players in a community; there is no boss instructing them what to do. I suspect that the need for shared purpose is an innate characteristic that spans species. The tendency to focus on individualism is artificial and counter-natural. The whole is greater than the sum of the parts is only true in presence of shared purpose.

If purpose answers what and why then values shape how, setting out what is expected and acceptable of people that work in an

---

[26] Team of Teams: New Rules of Engagement for A Complex World. General Stanley McChrystal (Retired)

organisation. Values are the core of the culture you want to create. In great companies, they are much more than posters on a wall. Great companies use them actively to guide decision making, including fundamental choices like who to hire, promote and fire; to determine priorities and to guide how processes are enacted. Recognise that you, as CEO, have a massive impact on how values are thought about across the company. Whilst no one expects you to be perfect, it is certain that no one respects a hypocrite. Your decisions, your actions, your words shape massively the culture of your company.

Many companies spend a lot of time in shaping the words that form their values and massively underinvest in the part that really matters, making them real. This is because the investment required is in a resource that is always in short supply: personal attention every day you are CEO. To bring your values to life you must:

- Explain how your actions and decisions are shaped by the values;

- Recognise, praise and promote people for demonstrating them;

- Sanction and remove people who consistently or significantly act against them;

- Design processes and measures that reflect and reinforce them;

- Make them central to your recruitment process.

The more I work with and study organisations, the more I recognise the importance of shared purpose and values. To think about them as a tick in the box exercise is to abdicate your primary role as a leader. They are among the most important things you will ever work on. Don't skimp on their development and, more importantly, bringing them to life in the decisions and actions you and your organisation take.

One final word: go back and re-read the example purpose statements above. All of them describe what the organisation does for its customers, not itself.

Agreement on ideal customers

When you start a business, you are desperate for customers – any customer. Whilst the need for revenue is understandable, a lack of focus is always a killer. Being clear about who you sell to and serve brings many benefits at any stage of your company:

- Product-market fit is easier to achieve;

- Marketing, sales, product and customer success work together better to a common goal;

- Pipeline conversion rates typically improve;

- Valuable resources can be focused on a tightly-defined cohort, increasing impact and productivity;

- Word of mouth is easier to generate and more impactful;

- CLTV improves as a result of lower early-stage churn.

Before I delve further into Ideal Customer Profile, let me share an example showing why they are so important to customer success.

I know well a company that believed selling to any company was good business: sales went after everything that moved. As a result, the company had very high first year churn, a significant percentage of which was down to customers that could never achieve value. Not only were they dissatisfied, but many were also downright angry and told everyone they could about it. Instead of delivering value, the company was dealing regularly with customers that wanted out of a 12-month contract that would never deliver for them. Sales knew they were signing up bad customers, but their metrics and commission drove them to do it.

Contrast that with the view of Greg Goldfarb, MD of SaaS VC Summit Partners. He says companies should "… *not accept a booking until customer has met a CS rep/accepted a CS plan and vice versa.*" [27] I disagree with the approach of having CS vet and approve sales but I'm convinced that the sentiment behind it is essential; dare I say, existential[28].

Company-wide agreement on ICP is a foundation on which a company-wide approach to customer focus is built. It is not a nice to have, it is a must have. Building this company-wide agreement and deep understanding of target customers is almost always the first piece of the jigsaw I seek to help my clients establish.[29]

An Ideal Customer Profile (ICP) has three elements:

- **Target companies**: A high level view of the types of companies you want to do business with. In addition to basics like industries, size, language and location, think about factors like life-stage, business model, culture, sophistication. The most important characteristics are likely to relate to the domain your product serves.

- **Role Profiles**: A detailed view of the specific people you want to sell to and will have to serve. I will address this element of the ICP further in Chapter Six.

---

[27] Venture Capital View of Customer Success: Aligning Software Vendor & Customer for Mutual Success. Presentation at Gainsight's Pulse 17

[28] I have implemented process that delivers an outline success plan to a prospect as part of the sales process. This ensures continuity across the customer lifecycle.

[29] The stage of your company's growth and maturity shapes the approach you need to develop your ICP. Early-stage companies testing product-market fit will use a qualitative, hypothesis-testing approach. Companies with established customer bases will adopt a more data-driven approach.

- **Situational factors**: These describe the conditions that indicate a customer is ready to take the next step. They apply across the customer lifecycle, not just new customer acquisition. Many of these factors will be specific to the domain your product serves and will differ by role. Macro- and micro-level situational factors can drive expansion revenue opportunities or trigger a churn risk. The common factor is that they indicate a context that requires a response.

In my experience, few B2B SaaS companies invest properly in building and maintaining ICPs. That does not mean you have to spend lots of money; the scarce resources here are commitment, intent and time to talk to customers. How can a B2B SaaS company claim to be committed to the success of its customers if it cannot describe in detail those two things: customers and their success? There is never a bad time to start building company-wide ICPs, so if you don't have them put this book down and start now!

Customer Engagement Blueprint

A CEO I was working with was concerned about customers telling him the challenges of doing business with his company, describing a "disjointed customer experience". My immediate response was "I'm not surprised. You haven't designed a joined-up experience for them."

The third element of organisation by design is a high-level (i.e. not detailed), outside-in design of the end-to-end customer lifecycle. This is the equivalent of the architect's overall blueprint. Its purpose is to provide an agreed view of the lifecycle of your chosen customers, into which experts supply their specialisms.

Building a Customer Engagement Blueprint requires input from people involved in all aspects of acquiring and serving customers: marketing, sales, customer success, services and product. Over a series of workshops, backed up by research, this cross-functional working group seeks answers to the following questions:

- What are the major challenges buyers face in acquiring and using your products?

- Who are the key people involved across the customer lifecycle?

- At each stage, what does success look like for the key people?

- How can you help them overcome their challenges?

Expressed properly, this "blueprint" does not constrain creativity, it enables it but channels it to a coherent design. I intentionally do not use the phrase "customer journey". The blueprint is a high-level view only. In my experience, attempts to define detailed customer journeys fail miserably, a point I will return to in Chapter Nine: "Their choice: not yours".

A Customer Engagement Blueprint takes aim at one of my pet hates: internally-focused, disconnected marketing, sales, product management and customer success processes. Most processes I have experienced describe what the company does, with scant regard for the customer. Allowing individual departments/teams to develop their own processes without an overarching blueprint leads to duplication, ineffective handovers and competing metrics: all hallmarks of ineffective organisations.

Measures

Even a good organisation can be screwed by bad measures. I don't think companies design measurement frameworks that intentionally create conflict; they just don't think about the bigger picture. That leaves a yawning gap for the law of unintended consequences to step in with a wrecking ball, especially when they are used as the basis of some element of compensation.

Yet again, mea culpa. I can recall all too many instances where I have made mistakes. They usually stem from the desire to have measures that relate closely to the work of an individual role, in the mistaken belief that individuals have direct control over outcomes. They rarely do; the wider system almost always hold sway. Even when the individual has some control, the benefits of focus are outweighed by the problems caused by losing sight of the purpose of the organisation.

Poor choice of measures can be extremely damaging, as this example from one company shows in spades.

Marketing's definition of a Marketing Qualified Lead (MQL) ensured they often delivered their target number of leads but with very low conversion rates, wasting marketing dollars in the process. Driven by a revenue-focused metric, they would argue with sales about who sourced a lead, as this drove commission. This created distrust and soaked up senior management time to sort out disputes.

Sales faced unrealistic quotas, complex commission structures and micro-management. Achieving quota was the only way a salesperson could develop to the next career step. This approach to measuring performance and compensation led salespeople to chase and close any business, including customers that could never achieve any meaningful benefit from using the product. It also created an environment where salespeople would, to put it in a positive light, stretch the truth to win the sale. It also drove massive discounting, making the average sale value ridiculously low.

You can guess the next problem. These bad fit customers were passed over to the CS team, often with little meaningful information. The customer quickly realised that they were unlikely to achieve value. In many cases, the first meaningful interaction with a CSM was a demand to cancel with a full refund. CS were blamed for and charged with having to sort out the fallout that all too often followed. The low average contract value (ACV) meant that delivering a meaningful success process ate up what little margin, if any, there was in the deal. CS earned a commission on renewal, but that was a fraction of what the salesperson earned on the same renewal even though they were not involved after the initial deal.

The company did acquire good fit customers, many of whom were great customers and advocates. With these customers, renewals, upsells and referrals were relatively easy to secure. CSMs used to love dealing with these customers. Unfortunately, the pernicious impact of the long tail of bad fit customers gnawed away at the confidence and engagement of CSMs, resulting in high staff turnover.

Many of the problems were driven by the disconnected way the different teams were measured and compensated. Giving someone a number to chase and paying them based on it will drive behaviours that help them maximise their earnings. They become the company's heroes: the people others seek to emulate because they are the favoured ones, both financially and by dint of management recognition. Achieving their reward and recognition takes priority above what is best for the company, cooperation with others and even behaving ethically.

Consider how behaviours might change if everyone in the organisation shared a common purpose and agreed a high-level engagement lifecycle and measures. What if variable compensation paid everyone based on the same measures that reflect the success of the organisation as a whole, not just a part of it? This is what I did at Clicktools. Everyone had the same bonus plan, based on the same simple formula: revenue growth x customer satisfaction.[30] If everyone focuses on the same measures, the discussion shifts from "what's best for me" to "what's best for us". It encourages collaboration rather than competition. Understand also that narrowly focused metrics constrain people's scope to be creative in how they properly achieve their goals. Higher level measures aligned to the company's overall goals provide scope for people to try different ways to achieve them.

A focus on common, high-level measures does not remove the need for extensive metrics and data points, many of which will be activity or

---

[30] Depending on the maturity and growth stage of the company, measures such as Customer Lifetime Value/CAC ratio and Net Revenue Retention better represent the whole customer lifecycle and the work of the whole organisation. LTV/CAC ratio introduces a productivity element, which becomes more important as growth scales, although NRR is increasingly recognised as the key driver of enterprise valuations.

department specific. Data is needed to understand how the prospect/customer is moving through the engagement lifecycle; how different individuals are performing and how processes are working. In my experience, there is a relationship between the ability to drive improvements and the quantity and quality of data available to them.

Soft capabilities

The success of your organisation is rarely the result of your organisation chart. Companies that excel develop capabilities that are often considered intangible and as a result often don't receive the attention they should. As CEO, you must figure out how you balance two things: creating the space for people to contribute expertise and ideas, which is essential for meaningful engagement, and the need to keep everyone working to the same ends.

There are five essential soft capabilities you need to harness to your purpose and nurture as you grow:

- Decision making;
- Goal setting and planning;
- Alignment;
- Collaboration;
- Autonomy.

You have to design an approach for each that suits your company and works in concert and is coherent with your purpose and values. For example, Amazon's "Working Backwards"[31] sets out an approach to building a business case that starts with the customer; a reflection of their mission "to be the earth's most customer-centric company". Google's adoption of OKRs,[32] with a focus on quarterly goals and

---

[31] You can find a description of Working Backwards, as described by Ian McAllister, a Director at Amazon, at https://www.quora.com/What-is-Amazons-approach-to-product-development-and-product-management

achievements, reflects two of its core values: "It's best to do one thing really, really well" and "Fast is better than slow".[33] Basecamp's product development process[34] takes a novel approach to prioritising features to be built. Most companies keep a running backlog list, features that have been proposed but not yet made the cut. Basecamp replaces this ever-growing list with a six-weekly betting table where a limited number of pitches are considered. Each pitch has a time commitment, and stakeholders select the pitches they believe will have the greatest impact. If a pitch is not selected, it is rejected and not added to a backlog. Every betting table is a fresh start.

Building such capabilities is difficult because they often need you to change: many of the practices required to succeed in the start-up phase won't work as well as you grow. Starting a company means you are involved in everything and you know just about everything. Getting a small team aligned may be difficulty, but issues can often be sorted out by getting everyone in a room and talking (for which often read arguing) it through. What worked when you were a team of 5–50 won't work the same with a team of 500.

Autonomy is one area where some CEOs struggle, especially founder CEOs; I know I did. They keep their fingers in every pie and reserve decision making rights for themselves. Micro-managers hold their organisations back. They slow down decision making, suppress creativity and, most importantly, kill the engagement of people in their organisation. I have yet to meet anyone who says they really enjoy working for a micro-manager. Avoid becoming one at all costs. Autonomy, the freedom to make choices and do things their way, is key to getting the best out of people. Remember, you have hired the best, and the best know how to do their job better than you do. Your

[32] You can learn more about OKRs at https://www.whatmatters.com

[33] Google's ten values are listed in "How Google Works" by Eric Schmidt and Jonathan Rosenberg.

[34] https://basecamp.com/shapeup

role is to give them context: direction, the right tools and information, and then get the f**k out of their way! Purpose and values, Ideal Customer Profile and the Customer Engagement Blueprint are the core of the context you need to provide.

Organisation by design is perhaps the most significant lesson I learned and applied in my time as CEO of Clicktools and in my coaching and consulting work. My experience: you cannot start the work of purposeful organisation design too early. In fact, the longer you leave it the more difficult the task becomes as silos, narrowly focused metrics and departmental processes take hold. These manifestations of your culture shape the actions and attitudes of new hires. Being clear about vision and values and, most significantly, how you and your leadership colleagues enact them will establish a positive cycle of reinforcement.

Advice to CEOs

- Remember, things won't change by changing lines and boxes on an organisation chart. Real change comes from changing work, skills and rewards. Form follows function!
- Don't underestimate the power of shared purpose and values as tools to guide and set the tone for how things are done.
- Design everything from the viewpoint of how this helps your target customer AND delivers results for your company. Shallow thinkers accept trade-offs; deep thinkers find "and" answers.
- Build your soft capabilities muscle early: the more you let go, the more you will get back.

6: Principle Three – People not customers

B2B – business to business; one legal entity to another legal entity; supplier to customer. Hence the phrase customer success. Like many, I had long recognised the importance of focusing on people in the buying and use of B2B SaaS, but it wasn't until researching for this book that I recognised just how central they were to the whole concept of customer success.

The faceless customer

Whilst discussing aspects of psychology and customer success (more of that later in this chapter) with CS leader Morika Georgiova, I commented that this discipline should be called people success, not customer success. It was one of those "aha" moments where previously disconnected pieces of the puzzle came together. People, not companies, decide whether or not to buy your products, even though the invoice is in the name of their company. People, not companies, decide if your product has delivered the value they expect. People make the decision about renewing their subscription or cancelling. People make the choice to recommend your product to others or advise them to steer to well clear of it. People, not customers, do it all.

The focus on this faceless thing called "a customer" underpins much of what is practised in the name of customer success and its emphasis on the company, especially the obsession with ROI and a singular outcome. How many of the people that use your product are actually bothered about the ROI it delivers? All they want is to do their job better and easier; they have their own priorities and challenges to worry about without having to figure out contribution to the ROI of the many different products they use. ROI is a device invented by old style software companies to justify the massive prices they charge. Touted widely during the sales process, the claims often fade into the shadows once the ink on the contract is dry. By focusing on ROI, or some other singular outcome, we lose sight of the needs of individuals. People become a means by which the desired outcome is achieved; a cog in the hierarchy of milestones and activities needed to achieve a business outcome. Hardly a human-first approach to doing business.

"Ah, but," I hear you say; there's always an "ah, but". We don't focus on ROI, we help customers achieve their desired outcome. Whose desired outcome? say I. The customer's desired outcome comes the reply. Which customer's desired outcome? say I. The one who signed the order? The one who holds the budget? The one who made the case for your product? The one who uses the valuable data your product provides? The one who logs in every day? The folks in IT that do all the tricky integration that your product needs to make it work? Silence is all too often the response. The economic buyer is an important part of a buyer–supplier relationship; after all they sanction the purchase. If that purchase is not used effectively, they are not likely to achieve value and, therefore, less likely to renew. Buyers can hire but users fire a supplier.

Differentiating between the customer and people might sound semantic, but language is important. As long as we think about the customer (singular) we lose sight of the people whose working lives we need to improve. We build processes and systems to serve "the customer". So I propose we stop thinking about customer success and focus on people success.

In this context, people are all the different roles involved around which you build your approaches to value delivery and revenue management. It is why I believe the Role Profile is the most important part of an Ideal Customer Profile. To target individual roles effectively, ICPs must get very granular; specifically:

- Ensure your ICPs include detailed Role Profiles that describe the work, challenges, goals and metrics of the people that buy, use and benefit from your products;
- Develop a deep understanding of how each role perceives and measures value at each stage of the engagement lifecycle and how they measure the value your product delivers;
- Marketing, sales and success processes that address the different needs of the roles involved;

- Products that provide flows and content specific to individuals roles.

Many argue that this is overly complex; that it is not possible to meet the needs of individuals to this degree. I counter that with two arguments. First, if you are to achieve meaningful success, success which maximises the propensity to buy, renew and increase spend, you have to deliver measurable value to each role involved. Some roles may be more influential at different stages, but to assume only one person, the decision maker, has absolute power does not reflect the reality of most organisations. Second, focusing on the individual makes it easier to develop interventions that are effective and efficient. Content can be focused on the challenge of the role and the context they are operating in, building relationship strength. Yes, it takes work to build and enact that understanding, but think about the alternative. You build a business that has no meaningful focus on the people that matter; a business that accepts value delivery is only possible at a simplistic level.

Role Profile

The Role Profile is the heart of an ICP. It is where the detail sits; the detail that captures and describes a deep understanding of the people you deal with. Here's a simple template of the Role Profile element of an ICP.

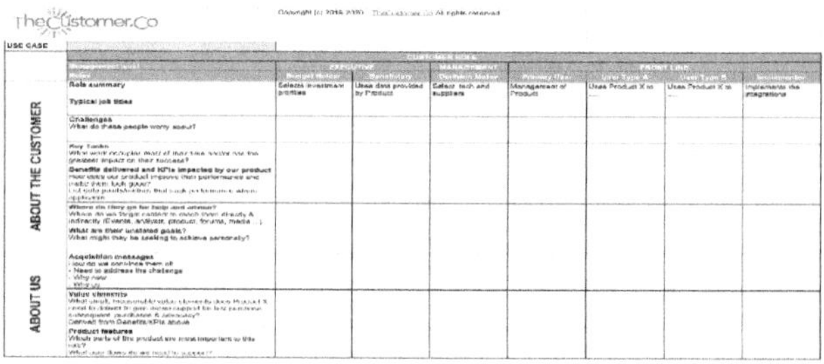

Fig 6.1: Template ICP Role Profile

73

The "About the Role [Customer]" section is where you must start. Much of what is required can't be gathered through surveys; it comes from rich conversations, sitting with them and watching them work. As they say in the region of the UK I hail from, "you have to live in their socks!" One of the keys to building an effective Role Profile is asking the right questions, looking for the right insights. The quality of questions is key.[35] The best questions are open and specific. Open in that they require the respondent to describe something rather than just say yes or no, or rank something. Specific in that the question focuses on an area of importance and, through chains of questions, digs deeper to uncover real issues.

The areas to dig into deepest are the role's work, challenges and KPIs. It is here that you will learn most about what they want to achieve. Not digging deep enough is a common mistake. Too often people shift focus into the "About Us" elements too early. It's an easy mistake to make: you know much more about "us" and you think you know enough about your customers. You might be an exception, but many do not know anywhere near enough.

A question I am often asked is, "Who should drive the building of an ICP and own it?" Shared ICPs are so fundamental that I place the responsibility for making this happen with you – the CEO. Whilst you may delegate the management of the project, you should ensure it happens, and that means giving your active support and involvement. You must corral teams across the company to ensure that it reflects customer needs across the customer engagement lifecycle. You have to secure the resources to both build and, more importantly, enact the ICPs. You also have to ensure that the resulting ICPs are widely accessible and used by all parts of the company.

I cannot stress enough the importance of detailed, shared Role Profiles as a foundation of company-wide focus on customer success.

---

[35] I can highly recommend Rob Fitzpatrick's book, "The Mom Test: How to talk to customers and learn if your business is a good idea when everybody is lying to you"

Psychology of customer success

Delivering success for individuals is only possible if you understand how people think, what motivates them, how they learn, what prevents them from making the steps need to achieve change. As an amateur psychologist (aren't we all) I recognise an immediate problem: a little knowledge can be a dangerous thing. That said, I think there are a few basics that can help; psychology 101 as it applies to customer focus.

The triune brain

Let's start with the organ that consumes more energy than any other part of the body. An idea first formulated by neuroscientist Paul MacLean, the triune (three part) brain is a simplified but basically accurate view of the structure of this amazing organ.

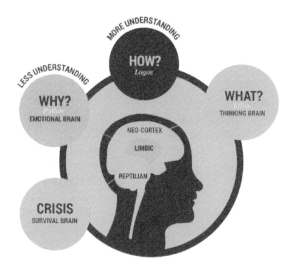

Fig 6.2: The triune brain

The three structures reflect the evolutionary development of the brain, which is broadly reflected in how the brain develops in a foetus growing in the womb. Here's a simplified summary of the function of each of the three parts.

The reptilian brain controls basic instinctive functions related to primitive survival issues such as exploration, feeding and aggression. These autonomic functions are so fundamental that we don't "think" about them – we just do them.

The limbic system, full of wonderful sounding structures like amygdala, hippocampus and hypothalamus, is the seat of our emotional and motivational systems, which shape how we respond (behave) to incoming stimuli. The limbic system is based on instincts and past experiences that influence our emotions and beliefs. It also affects motivation, learning and memory. It is the place where most of the cognitive biases, the shortcuts our brain uses to simplify life, are enacted.

The neocortex is the rational part of the brain where we reason, process logical arguments and develop ideas. It is the part of the brain that many believe is most advanced in humans and perhaps why we have become the dominant species.

The evolutionary and foetal development of the brain is mirrored by the way the brain processes information. Stimuli first hit the reptilian brain, which decides how our body responds: fight or flight and other autonomic responses. The limbic system then gets its hands on the information and applies a "values and beliefs" filter before the information hits the neocortex and the process of rational, logical decision making begins. The problem is that our limbic system messes with the information before passing it on. It filters it and assigns weight based on our pre-existing beliefs and values lodged in it. To make things even harder, it does this without telling us, because our limbic system operates predominantly in the subconscious. Of course, our rational, logical brain can overrule our emotions but only if it is aware, which is a challenge as all this thinking is happening subconsciously, literally without our awareness. There's even a phrase in neuroscience to describe it – the amygdala hijack!

In simplistic terms, we make decisions emotionally before we make them rationally: we select our logic based on our pre-existing values and beliefs. That's why understanding how we think is so important when we are talking about how we make people successful.

Cognitive biases

One area of psychology of particular value to building customer success capability is the field of cognitive biases. According to Wikipedia, a cognitive bias is "a systematic pattern of deviation from norm or rationality in judgment. Individuals create their own 'subjective reality' from their perception of the input." We are not the logical, rational people we often think we are. Shaped by hundreds of thousands of years of evolution, these subconscious shortcuts are instrumental in planning and decision making, even in the supposed logical and rational discipline of business.

Wikipedia lists a total of 194 cognitive biases , some of which are closely related to others and overlap significantly. They are listed under three headings (the number shows the quantity in each section):

- Decision making and belief biases (124);
- Memory biases (42);
- Social biases (28).

Some of these will be familiar through terms in regular use. "Jumping on the bandwagon", "groupthink" and "status quo" all give their names to or stem from cognitive biases. Operating in the subconscious, we are rarely aware of how they shape our thinking. They are so effective, one might say pernicious, because they operate subconsciously. They shape our decisions before we decide!

I have compiled a list of cognitive biases relevant to customer success with my view of the implication of that bias for customer success. To give you a flavour, here are some of my favourites.

NAME	DESCRIPTION	CS IMPLICATIONS
ANCHORING OR FOCALISM	The tendency to reply too heavily, or "anchor", on one trait or piece of information when making decisions (usually the first piece of information acquired on that subject)	When setting goals for a success plan, it is important to establish an expectation of what is reasonable and achievable very early on. Sales people that over promise can damage a future relationship before the deal is concluded because of this bias. This is one reason customer success has to be built into each stage of the engagement cycle
ATTENTIONAL BIAS	The tendency of perception to be affected by recurring thoughts	Say, say it again and say it again! Repetition is often an effective way of embedding learning. Content and resources that repeat at different stages reinforce the message. Of course, to be effective the repetition has to be contextually rich to the recipient otherwise it is just pestering.
CURSE OF KNOWLEDGE	When better-informed people find it extremely difficult to think about problems from the perspective of lesser-informed people.	Expertise has to be projected and explained in ways that is relative to the recipient. Even for the same role, we have to understand the different levels of sophistication and tailor our communication and interventions accordingly. It is why deep role profiles aas part of ICPs are so important.
DEFAULT EFFECT	When given a choice between several options, the tendency to favor the default one.	Proscriptive customer success works! Most people don't like to have to think so will take a default position if they can see how it relates to them. Again, the individual's context matters when we are building success interventions.
PRESENT BIAS	The tendency of people to give stronger weight to payoffs that are closer to the present time when considering trade-offs between two future moments.	We are more likely to help customers change in a series of small steps. Large scale outcomes can seem distant and therefore unachievable. Little and often is often a more effective change strategy.
SUBADDITIVITY EFFECT	The tendency to judge the probability of the whole to be less than the probability of its constituent parts.	Focus on big goals or desired outcomes can be counter-productive. Presenting change in small chunks is seen as lower risk and therefore more likely to succeed.
SEMMELWEIS REFLEX	The tendency to reject new evidence that contradicts a paradigm.	People are wedded to their world view. We have to understand an individual's stance on issues if we are to be effective in communicating with them

Fig 6.3: Selected cognitive biases and their implications for customer success

I have come to the conclusion that a basic understanding of psychology is core to delivering success to the people called customers. It is essential to shaping effectively the interventions you design to deliver success for customers. It is why reference to cognitive biases are included as an item to be considered when building success processes. I will return to this in the next chapter.

There is a second, equally pressing reason for building psychology knowledge: to shape the products you build. B2B SaaS businesses are, at their heart, suppliers of product, the natural extension of which is that the product is the primary vehicle for delivering success. I will explore in depth this important topic in Chapter Ten: "Code scales better than people".

Advice to CEOs

- Build a deep understanding of the people you sell to and serve. It was part of your thinking when you started the company so stick with it. Lead by example by meeting regularly with customers and prospects and not just around deals. It will deliver real benefits.

- Lead the development and application of rich Role Profiles. Make sure they are used by all relevant teams. You look across the whole company and it's your job to make sure the company pulls together on this.

- Review your acquisition messaging and success processes to identify changes that will improve your focus on individuals.

- Become an amateur psychologist and think about how customers think. Use this knowledge in your messaging, product and value delivery processes. If you keep the needs of customers to the fore and avoid exploitative uses, your customers will achieve greater success and you will increase their propensity to buy, renew and grow.

7: Principle 4 – Build a deep understanding of value

Outcome, value, goals, success. These are all words used to describe what people are seeking by using your products. Which term you use is less important than what actions you take to deliver it to customers. My preference is value.

Why is the delivery of value so important to your B2B SaaS company? As I have previously explained, it is the basis of everything your company does: the value proposition, the product, marketing and sales messaging and, of course, customer success capabilities must all focus on communicating and delivering value to your chosen customers. It is the fundamental reason a customer buys and continues to do business with you. The greater the value you deliver, the more you become a "need to have" rather than a "nice to have" product. Value, stickiness and your revenue correlate.

The value equation

A failure to explain and deliver value removes the fundamental reason for people to buy and continue to use your product. If they cannot see value and are not continually getting the value they expected or were promised, or are having to work too hard to achieve that value, then why would they continue to buy? This simple equation describes the factors at play in their propensity to buy and renew:

Propensity to buy, renew and expand =

(need for value x value achieved)/effort

Let me explain each of them.

First, **propensity to buy, renew and expand.** Propensity is all you can assess. There are no guarantees that even if you get everything right, you will get the initial sale, the renewal or growth. You can, however, significantly improve your chances, increase propensity, if you do the right things the right way. I use the word propensity for a second reason; it is a nod to the realisation that buying, like almost any decision, has an emotional element to it. It is how people perceive the different elements that matters. That perception will be shaped by the rational element but significantly conditioned by what they think about you and your company.

Need for value is about recognising that people have many challenges. Winning and retaining a customer is therefore dependent on helping them recognise the need and its importance relative to other options.

This is not about your product and its merits but about the buyer's perception of the relative impact of different problems or opportunities. Again, this is about understanding individuals, not a company. Depending on context, this is about answering different questions:

- Why change: what is this problem/opportunity, and does it affect me?
- Why now: why do I need to address this now?
- Why you: why are you the right people to help me?
- Why stay: why should I continue to buy your product?
- Why more: why should I buy more or other things from you?

Their success – their perception of the value they achieve – is the red thread that runs through this dialogue. That dialogue can only begin when the customer prioritises change in the domain your product addresses. In this respect, competition is not other providers but the other challenges that compete for resources and mindshare. The route to winning is value-focused messaging and processes built on a deep understanding of the different people you sell to and serve.

Value achieved, like beauty, is in the eye of the beholder, and in any B2B SaaS product there are likely to be many beholders. Different individuals perceive and prioritise different needs, and even where the recognition of need is common, how it is manifested and how they measure its impact differs. There is, therefore, no such thing as a single outcome. Each of the key roles you serve have different expectations of the value to be achieved by doing business with you.

Effort is a measure of the work and resources needed to achieve the value they expect. In this context, effort is a multi-faceted thing, comprising:

- Financial effort – how much will it cost to purchase and implement your product and any associated changes;
- Time effort – the person days required to implement and the elapsed time to achieve value;
- Reputational effort – how the value achieved improves/risks my standing with colleagues and other stakeholders;
- Intellectual effort – how much mental capacity is needed to make the change.

When it comes to return on effort, human nature is contradictory. Deep down, we know that meaningful change is often hard work, achieved only with real effort, but at the same time we prefer the easy path, the quick fix. Recognise that lowering the perception of effort to achieve value will increase your customer's propensity to buy; a series of small steps are perceived as easier to achieve than one large step.

Reducing effort also means your product must be ridiculously easy to use, providing the help and guidance people need at every step; cajoling them to do what is needed and reinforcing their progress. It is also about how you think about and present value differently to the different people involved.

Effort is also shaped by the individual's sophistication in the problem/opportunity your product serves. People and companies with deep and broad knowledge may find it easier and quicker to implement and create value with your product compared to those who are less knowledgeable or experienced. Understanding this sophistication is an important aspect of your ICP that shapes how you enable the customer to achieve value. Minimising effort, removing friction and focusing on value at all stages of the customer lifecycle are the keys to shifting the value–effort ratio.

One thread runs, unseen, through the equation: the decisions are all made by individuals – people, not customers. It is vital, therefore, to build a deep understanding of value at the level of the individual, the key roles you serve, not the organisation.

Understanding value

You cannot deliver something you don't understand. The first step, therefore, is building a deep understanding of how the different characteristics of value inter-relate. I call this a Value Framework.

Whilst the framework looks simple (it is), populating it with meaningful data is a challenge. It is a challenge because it requires a very deep understanding of the people you serve and how your product enables them in <u>measurable</u> ways. In my experience, it is a depth of understanding few SaaS companies have built.

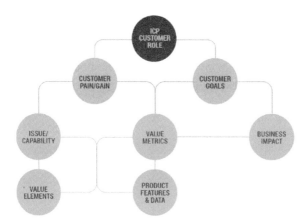

Fig 7.1: Value Framework

The Value Framework begins with the individuals you serve: specifically the role, the pain/gain they want to focus on and their goals. The pain/gain relates to different issues and capabilities your product addresses. For example, if your product is about lead generation, issues may be about content strategy, social campaigns or paid advertising. Each of these issues/capabilities can be tracked by one or more value metrics, which if improved have a measurable impact on the business. Value metrics (leading indicators) and business impact (lagging indicators) are how you show the customer you have helped them achieve their goals. Value Elements contain the advice and guidance you provide to help your customers address the issues/capabilities that resolve their pain/gain points.

These Value Elements will often relate to how to use the features and data in your product but will also go "beyond product" and provide advice and guidance around processes, metrics and skills the role should consider.

Building and populating this framework helps identify gaps in understanding, provides a structure for collating resources and is a great tool for helping new hires understand your company's value proposition. More importantly, it is something every part of your company can and should use. It sets out the basis of a value-based messaging framework for marketing; helps sales develop role specific tools and conversations; provides the basis for value enablement plans and, of course, guides product managers as they productise the value enablement process. In the context of product-enabled value, it describes the structures you need to build.

The problem with outcomes

Our understanding of the need to focus on value has progressed significantly in recent years. Paul Henderson's excellent book *The Outcome Generation*[36] explains the importance of focusing on success outcomes, not just the outcome delivered by the product. In the book, Paul describes a success outcome as "*an ongoing business result the top management of the customer would regard as a success*". Much of the work on understanding and implementing outcomes-based selling and success has been driven by suppliers focused on larger enterprise software implementations. Large purchases need to promise large returns to justify them. It's why, understandably, many pursuing

---

[36] The Outcome Generation: How a New Generation of Technology Vendors Thrives Through True Customer Success. Paul Henderson ISBN:9780648216100

outcomes-based thinking focus on the company and the needs of top management. In doing so, however, individuals get overlooked in favour of the faceless customer.

I recognise the importance of outcomes but believe how the thinking is implemented in most organisations misses two important points.

As I explained in Chapter Two, "A singular, high-level goal is often distant from the vast majority of people using the application". A digital marketer looks for ways to make their job easier and deliver more and better leads. They probably have minimal, if any, interest in the financial ROI of the products they use to do their job. Atomisation of the buyer brings this gap forward into the acquisition cycle, where the mindset is often "I need to do this now and get results tomorrow." This reinforces (and is reinforced by) my belief that individuals, not companies, should be the primary focus of our efforts to deliver success. If outcomes were so important and useful, ROI calculators would not be forgotten after the sale, which most are – by both the supplier and the buyer.

Second, success outcomes focus on a single plan, breaking down a singular goal into tasks and milestones. A single plan ensures everyone does what they should, with a project manager keeping people on track; or so the theory goes. This mechanistic approach is rarely effective when irrational, emotional people are the conduit through which results are achieved: people who have their own priorities and preferences for how they work. People are the reason why most change plans fail; specifically a lack of commitment to an outcome they don't recognise as relevant to them.

This disconnected relationship between a singular outcome and the preference of individuals is why many companies struggle to deliver results with an outcomes-based approach. A singular outcome often makes implementation seem like a massive challenge (remember the subadditivity effect cognitive bias). The pull of the status quo suddenly seems preferable to tackling a large change programme. The singular business outcome also lacks the granularity needed to make meaningful interventions with the individuals involved in buying, using and assessing the contribution of your product. Whilst outcomes have been a step forward in thinking, I think we can, and should, go further. There is a different and I think better approach based on delivering smaller chunks of value focused on the needs and performance of individuals. I call these **Value Elements**: an approach grounded in the work and ambitions of individuals rather than the companies they work for.

Introducing Value Elements

Value Elements are to customer success what micro-services are to software architectures.[37] The old approach to software involved building a single, monolithic program. The micro-services approach structures an application as a set of autonomous, independently deployable capabilities. Martin Fowler, a recognised micro-services expert says, "*These services are built around business capabilities and independently deployable by fully automated deployment machinery. There is a bare minimum of centralized management of these services ...*"[38] Note that last sentence.

Rather than a single, monolithic outcome for "the customer", Value Elements are a library of small-scale value, independently deployable. Focusing on the success of individuals and the context they face at a point in time creates pockets of success, which when aggregated deliver meaningful change. This shift of emphasis leads to a shift of effort: more time is spent on improving performance and less on planning and coordinating. Creating these pockets of small-scale success may seem chaotic but as a former colleague used to tell me

---

[37] IT architectures have a parallel history with dominant organisation models of the time. Centralised bureaucracies were dominant at the time of mainframe computing; mini-computing supported the growth of business unit/decentralised businesses; networks grew alongside the internet and web. Now, micro-systems and APIs are enabling the growth of ecosystems.

[38] https://www.martinfowler.com/articles/microservices.html

constantly, *"Don't worry David; it will all come together like a well-oiled slick."* Mechanistic thinkers may struggle with this "laissez-faire" approach, but nature provides many examples of organisations that thrive when individual players act in furtherance of a shared purpose.[39]

A value element is an incremental improvement addressing the needs of a specific role for a given context. Think of it as the minimum value that must be delivered for the customer to want to move to the next step in their buying process or actions to gain some benefit from using your product.

Value Elements differ from success outcomes in two ways. First, they are much more granular. This better reflects the need to respond to the atomisation of the buyer, their desire for rapid value and the likelihood of success. A Value Element's relationship to the needs of a specific role shifts the focus from the organisation to an individual/team. It is also much more closely related to their context.

This tighter focus also reflects a second difference: the independence of each Value Element from others. Remember, outcome thinking is borne out of the need to justify large enterprise-wide software implementations. Many such software projects failed because these cases were artificial. Whereas outcomes are built in a hierarchical model, Value Elements are more akin to natural systems.

Value Elements play well to the psychology of customer success. For example, the contrast effect and distinction bias suggest we notice when something has changed and are influenced by the direction of change. The hyperbolic discounting bias suggests that we favour the immediate over the delayed and distant. In other words, progress towards a smaller goal is more visible and motivating than the same

---

[39] Here's a couple of examples to trigger your thinking. Termite mounds are highly sophisticated constructions that are constantly renewed and extended. Which termite is the architect or project manager? Shoals of fish can have tens of thousands of members, but which fish makes the decision to change direction? Whilst they exist, hierarchies are not the predominant basis of order in nature.

quantum of progress to achieving a bigger goal. A number of cognitive biases suggest we prefer quick and simple over complicated, even if the complicated thing is ultimately a better use of time and energy. Complex problems make it difficult for us to store and process the quantity of information associated with them, so we tend to focus on what we think is important.

Value Elements have the following characteristics:

- They describe the work, challenges, metrics, enabling resources and rationale for successfully completing a task or simple goal;
- Different levels of advice and goals are included in a Value Element to cater for the difference in sophistication of the people exploiting it;
- Data, overlaid with personal choice, determine which value element an individual selects;
- A value element relates to one or more roles and one or more use cases;
- Deployment of Value Elements may repeat with increasing levels of achievement;
- Deployment of Value Elements is often not linear;
- A Value Element is independent of others but when their impact is aggregated they deliver substantive performance improvements;
- Each Value Element can be tracked to determine progress and level of achievement.

Value Elements across the customer lifecycle

A Value Element describes what it takes for an individual to successfully complete a task or achieve a goal. Whist many think of value delivery as a post-sale activity, I contend that it permeates the whole journey. Good marketing and sales communicate the value your product enables; great marketing and sales enhance the buyers' capabilities, add new knowledge and skills or make their work easier and better. Value Elements are, therefore, applicable across the entire customer lifecycle.

I use a simple structure for Value Elements:

- An explanation of what has to be done and why, both in terms of using the product and other "beyond product" changes and actions. These enabling resources might take the form of guided steps, tooltips, videos or links to other resources. The goal is to keep the initiation and as much of the delivery in-app as is possible. An important but oft overlooked aspect of help is to explain why the actions are needed: how the action relates to the value they are seeking.

- A way of measuring the result – value metrics. These may be generated from data within the app, captured through integrations or, as a last resort, entered by the user. Tracking progress against value metrics is essential to prove value achieved to the individuals using the app. Reporting progress may also extend to key roles that are not users.

- The **minimum** prerequisites: what other Value Elements **must** be completed before this can be tackled. Beware of imposing too many limitations and thus falling into the parent–child "we know what's best for you" relationship trap.

Some Value Elements already exist. Marketing, sales, customer success and product will all have resources designed to help people. Curating existing resources, aligning them to specific roles and tasks people face and ensuring the value message is consistent, is the first step in building your library of Value Elements.

Iterative value delivery

Breaking value down into small, contextually-focused chunks changes the nature of the value delivery process. In place of a single monolithic success plan focused on a single outcome, value delivery becomes an iterative cycle. The individual selects the pain/gain(s) they want to address, the performance goal(s) they want to achieve and off they go! You supply advice and guidance to help them achieve manageable goals, track their activities and report on performance improvements at both the individual and aggregate level. Rinse and repeat. Some people may choose to tackle multiple Value Elements consecutively; some may repeat the same activity with constantly improving levels of performance. if the performance in a particular pain/gain point slips, it might be revisited.

In this iterative approach, there is no master plan, no project manager and no fixed timeline. In its place are rich context, individual choice and, I argue, greater engagement. It's an approach that gives greater autonomy to individualism, which is known to be an important driver of motivation.

One argument levelled at the idea of Value Elements and iterative value delivery is that whilst it is fine for software implemented by individuals or teams, it doesn't work for big ticket, large scale, enterprise-wide system implementations where usage is mandated. I disagree. The underlying philosophy of focus on the individual, continuing iterative value cycles and context driven implementation apply whatever the scale. The only difference is the number of roles, pain/gain points and individuals. The more complex the implementation, the more a Value Elements approach is appropriate. Large projects impose a proportionately higher project management overhead. Adopting Value Elements removes most of this, replacing it with an iterative approach to value delivery. That said, there is one area where a linear planned approach is needed. Initial installation and configuration often require tasks to be done in a particular order. This does not mean the same approach is appropriate beyond setup.

Go back to the list setting out the characteristics of Value Elements and ask yourself a simple question: "Is this applicable to achieving value for the different people who buy and use your products?" When they have applied this test, most recognise the validity of the approach. What's holding them back is often their existing paradigm of outcomes and customer success.

Case study

Technical SEO is a complex subject with an increasingly important role to play in customer acquisition as paid search costs continue to rise. Deepcrawl is a leader in this field, counting many of the world's largest web-centric businesses as customers. Deepcrawl rebuilt its approach to success planning to focus on delivering iterative, measurable value to key roles, which span from deep domain experts to Chief Marketing Officers.

The work started with building a Value Framework using the model set out above[40]. This was built as an app which makes it easy for anyone in Deepcrawl to understand the needs of key roles and the problems they face in building SEO performant websites. Each of these issues is tracked by one or more value metrics, which in turn relate to measures of business impact. These leading and lagging indicators help Deepcrawl guide different roles in customer prioritise projects. The app is used across the company to:

- Act as a central repository of customer understanding;

- Help new starters understand the challenges Deepcrawl customers face and how the company addresses them;

- Help sales, customer success and professional services identify solutions and position messaging for different customer challenges;

- Link to resources that can be used across the customer engagement lifecycle, improving the ability to provide context-rich content.

[40] Credit and thanks to Matt Ford of Deepcrawl for his excellent work in applying the ideas and building their Value Framework.

As the Value Framework is rolled out, more and more resources are being added, building the company's ability to share best practices.

The end of outcomes?

Does the introduction of Value Elements mean the end of outcomes? Yes ... and no.

Value Elements enable individuals to achieve something important to them at a point in time: the next step on their journey. When aggregated, each step makes a significant impact on the performance of the customer's business. But what if everyone is doing what they want? What if they are not "on message" and not shooting for the same goal? This is where outcome as vision comes into play. Rather than set a singular goal backed up by an all-embracing success plan, help your customers describe a vision, a future state, and then help people get on with achieving it. This is very different from planning for specific outcomes. Visions are not plans. They provide direction without prescribing actions. The same is true of outcome as vision. Paul Henderson [ibid] recognises this with the concept of to-be states.

If you really know your stuff and have a deep understanding of the people you sell to and serve, you will have something valuable to say about what this future looks like; something they will value and subscribe to. You can help them shape their vision and, in so doing, carve a place for your company in their future. Tien Tzuo talks about the "three rooms" framework.[41]' framework. Room one tells the market what's happening in the world and why they need to do something about it. Room two articulates the value available and room three talks about your product. Tzuo adds that most companies "are missing a foundational thesis": they lack a room one story. More importantly, the three rooms framework ties the vision for your company to the vision and value you paint for your chosen customers. Helping them paint their vision helps you achieve yours.

---

[41] Subscribed: Ibid.

Advice to CEOs

- Build a task force to build out a Value Framework as a repository for the deep understanding of the people you sell to and serve as the basis for identifying Value Elements.
- Require teams across the engagement lifecycle to develop resources to support the implementation of Value Elements.
- Review your tech stack and its ability to deliver Value Elements.
- Lead from the front by always asking; "How does this help us better understand and deliver value to our chosen customers?"
- Develop and communicate your vision for the key roles in your target customers.

8: Principle 5 – Success is selling

The central thesis of the book is that customers' success, the value your product delivers for people in your chosen customers, is the red thread that runs through your B2B SaaS company. It is everything your company does to win, satisfy, retain and grow your chosen customers. Value is why people buy. Value is the basis of renewal and expansion. Value drives positive word of mouth. Value, as measured by the customer, is at the heart of everything and everything includes selling.

Value as the primary sales tool

Your customers' focus on value, as they define it, is taking on greater significance as a result of changes I have discussed. SaaS makes it easier[42] to swap out products that are not performing and, in many domains, there are an increasing number of options. Stickiness by inertia is still an advantage for the incumbent but less so. The COVID crisis drove many companies to review their software spend, keeping "must have" and dumping "nice to have" products. Categorisation was based primarily on value delivered. If executives are not hearing howls of protest from users backed up by performance data from across the user base, the default is that product is a nice to have. **Success is selling!**

As I discussed in Chapter Two, freemium and free trial shifts the original SaaS sales process of "See -> Try -> Buy" to "See -> Try -> Value -> Buy", meaning delivering value is increasingly a "pre-sales" activity. If the individuals that use your product don't get the value they expect, they don't buy. If they don't buy, you lose any potential viral or

---

[42] Easier does not <u>always</u> mean simple. Replacing any software often involves costs of learning, when productivity might dip. Even here, increasingly easy-to-use SaaS products are eating into the learning curve, further reducing barriers to switching. SaaS typical means shorter contract terms and more points in time when a decision is actively reviewed. That said, to assume frictionless switching is a mistake.

advocacy benefits: land and expand never lands. In this "deliver or die" environment, no value means no sale. **Success is selling!**

In an excellent article,[43] investor Rav Dhaliwal said, *"there is no such thing as post sales but rather there is the first sale with a customer, the next sale with them and so on ..."* He explains that selling should be viewed as a repeating cycle of value delivery and next sale – renewal, upsell or advocacy. I believe it is a mistake to see value delivery and selling as separate motions: the former drives the latter. I use the metaphor of the double helix of DNA and its role in reproduction. The first strand of the double helix is value enablement. As value grows, it creates bonds to your revenue. Each element of value strengthens the link with revenue. For example, improving value metrics strengthens renewal propensity; addressing additional pain/gain points creates upsell opportunities and improving the metrics that matter improves relationships with individuals, creating a willingness to advocate. The message is simple: you don't get the revenue unless you can prove the value. **Success is selling!**

Outcomes-based selling is the latest in a long-line of methodologies being touted as the answer to improving sales. I believe outcomes-based selling is crucial; I just question how new it really is. I also have concerns where a focus on value is implemented by one function in isolation. This just increases the risk of fragmentation across the customer lifecycle. The key is to ensure that this is not an isolated process but part of a purposefully designed, joined-up engagement lifecycle. As CEO, you have to recognise that value is a company-wide capability.

Don't sell; nurture buying

Jay Simons, former President of Atlassian, says *"Software should be bought, not sold."* [44] Selling is the process of uncovering needs and

---

[43] https://medium.com/@ravsterd/theres-no-such-thing-as-post-sales-a2dd1bfb3efc

showing people how they can, with the aid of your product, address those needs. To me, that sounds much like a customer success mindset where the core question is always, "How can I help this individual achieve their next goal?" I describe this selling by helping approach as nurturing buying, which I freely recognise will be seen as semantics to many. I make the differentiation because it strengthens the focus on the customer/buyer and the value they achieve, which is the core of a successful B2B SaaS business.

The dictionary defines the noun nurture as "*to care for and protect (someone or something) while they are growing*", which perfectly describes the underlying sentiment; helping buyers/customers learn and improve, which I believe represents the best traditions of selling. Care and protect includes not selling to people who you cannot help, although that does not exclude persuading people that they face issues they may not have yet identified.

Nurturing buying starts with the context of the individual, suggests next steps and helps them to achieve it. By relating your customers' pain/gain points to the capabilities of your product, you tie together customer value and revenue streams. I liken this to the double helix of DNA where the two main strands are your value delivery and revenue management processes. The connecting bonds are repeatable and measurable delivery of value, which strengthen relationships between you and the people your serve. Whilst many think this work comes after the initial sale, I believe it starts in the acquisition phase. For each step the buyer has to take, your first question is "How we can help them?" Chris Savage, CEO of video marketing software supplier Wistia, seems to agree, saying: "*In essence, our sales approach isn't that different from our customer success approach. In both cases, we're just helping people get the most out of our products. It's just that one group helps existing customers and one group helps prospects.*" [45] I would add that success is selling!

---

[44] Quoted at HubSpot's INBOUND conference 2019.

[45] https://openviewpartners.com/blog/embracing-sales-in-a-

The iterative approach to value delivery discussed in Chapter Seven has implications for how you nurture buying and the shape of the pipeline. As B2B SaaS shifted its emphasis from churn prevention to growth, depicting the pipeline shifted from a funnel to a dickie-bow. This reflected the importance of revenue generated after the first sale but missed what Rav Dhaliwal calls the continuous sales motion (ibid). An iterative, continuous value delivery process throws off iterative upsell opportunities, which requires a much better and wider understanding of the links between pain/gain points, measurable value and product capabilities. This makes the pipeline more akin to a belt buckle than a dickie-bow. The initial acquisition motion, where value is the basis of the pitch, is followed by the buckle, repeating iterations of value and revenue growth opportunities. Done well, this generates the point of the belt, positive word of mouth that creates secondary revenue. This secondary revenue is typically low cost, fast to convert and generates higher retention than other sources.

FUNNEL   DICKIE-BOW   BELT

Fig 8.1 From funnel to belt

The top of the funnel remains similar, with marketing and product generating leads, but thereafter, the process changes. First, the need for rapid time to value brings the value discovery and delivery process into the initial acquisition phase. In a product-led acquisition process a "See -> Try -> Value -> Buy" motion is embedded in the product. In a more traditional sales process, the key is inclusion of a mutually agreed, high level value delivery statement, setting out a vision as outcome and the initial pain/gain points to be addressed for the key

product-led-company/

customer roles. This becomes the basis of the first weeks of the relationship. Thereafter, the iterative nature of value delivery creates iterative opportunities to reinforce the value and therefore the case for renewal and, where appropriate, trigger upsell opportunities.

CS and revenue

It is impossible to explore success as selling without talking about the uneasy relationship many in the CS profession have with revenue. There is a large and vocal school of thought that commercial responsibility is at odds with the need to focus on value delivery and doing the right thing for the customer; that any involvement in commercial activities threatens the efficacy of the trusted advisor role. They argue that commercial responsibility introduces a conflict of interest, especially when some form of variable pay is linked to it.

Let me pin my colours to the mast: given that customer success (value to customers) is the basis of everything the company does; customer success is a commercial activity and those working in it need a commercial mindset and skillset.

Trust underpins buying. When buying, your customer expects you to do the right thing for them and deliver on the promises you make. A focus on understanding value on their terms and helping achieve it builds trust. To assume that only someone focused on one part of the relationship, customer success, is the driver of trust is a fallacy. The goal is not to get the customer to trust one or two individuals but to trust your entire organisation. This is best achieved by projecting a deep understanding of the needs of your chosen customers and showing how you address them across the entire lifecycle. Important though they are, individual relationships are only one part of trust building; as important is knowing what promises to make when and knowing how to repeatedly deliver on them.

Many of the problems with recognising CS as a commercial activity arise from measures and compensation; specifically, believing selling must be quota-driven with commission-based compensation plans. It is argued that the best salespeople are money driven and only by holding out this golden carrot will they perform. There are fundamental problems with this argument.

Those that point out the correlation between high performers assume that pay is <u>the causal driver</u> of performance. Numerous research studies into motivation of knowledge workers[46] show that extrinsic motivation, in this case money, is only effective in the short term. Over time, it is viewed as an essential part of the package and shifts from earned to required in the minds of the recipient. Even sales experts recognise this. Sales assessment specialists Objective Management Group say: *"If we look at the data from the 450,000 salespeople that have been assessed by Objective Management Group, the percentage of findings showing lack of money motivation, especially among higher income earners, has been increasing each year. It's not that they aren't money motivated anymore, as much as they aren't as money motivated as they were earlier in their career, when their money motivation got them to their current income level."* [47]

Second, most people in the company are not paid commission. Does that mean they don't work as hard or care as much about their performance? I suspect not. Many of these people are behind important ideas and innovations; they share their experience, coach others and deliver results every day. Lack of variable pay or a bonus does not prevent them doing a good, often a great, job.

Finally, selling is a team activity and never the result of what one person or role does. Try selling when there is no one to deliver the product or service, when nobody is generating demand or providing supporting material. It's possible but only in a solo-entrepreneur business. Paying sales commission to one group of people undermines

---

[46] Daniel Pink's book *Drive: The surprising truth about what motivates us* quotes several research studies about the effectiveness of money as a motivator.

[47] https://www.peaksalesrecruiting.com/blog/are-sales-reps-motivated-by-money/

the teamwork inherent in the success of any organisation. I have seen it happen.

There is no rule in the business handbook that says sales has to be commission-based, and a number of companies are turning their backs on this practice. One is CultureAmp, led by Didier Elzinga. Didier points out that there is no proven research or theory that backs up the effectiveness of commission-based sales compensation. His own experience shows that no-commission sales compensation does work and that commission-based sales is damaging, with one group getting the benefit of an outcome only possible from a team working together. Didier also talks about "mission not commission"; the importance of giving people a sense of purpose for their work.[48] Graham Hawkins, CEO of Sales Tribe and author of *The Future of the Sales Profession*, sums it up well. *"Let's cut to the chase: sales quotas and commissions are completely at odds with customer success, and if you are one of those businesses that proudly exclaims that you are 'customer centric' whilst continuing to measure and reward your sales performance primarily around revenue attainment, then you are being totally disingenuous, and your business is now at risk."* [49]

This is not to say that money is unimportant. It is crucial, but as the work of psychologists Maslow and Herzberg points out, while the lack of money can be a demotivator, beyond a certain point money itself is not a motivator. Most people, including those in sales, respond to higher order factors such as challenging work, recognition for one's achievements, responsibility, the opportunity to do something meaningful, involvement in decision making and a sense of importance. Money is a short-hand way of assessing these factors but only because societies have chosen it as a proxy of success.

---

[48] Quoted in the SaaStr Podcast #102: Didier Elzinga, Founder & CEO @ CultureAmp On Why You Should Not Pay Your Sales Team Commission

[49] https://www.salesforlife.com/blog/no-commissions-no-quota-the-future-model-for-sales/

I contend, therefore, that the core problem is not with the concept of value-based selling but a failure of how it is implemented, which is an organisation design challenge.

Advice to CEOs

- Review the messaging you use across the customer engagement lifecycle to ensure it is consistent in its focus on the value you create for customers. Focus on how you can help people at every stage.

- Build a Value Framework to help people understand the relationship between pain/gain points and your products' capabilities as the basis for nurturing buying.

- Mine your experiences to understand the triggers that help you identify potential upsell opportunities. Ensure your sales and customer success teams know how to recognise and respond to them.

- Critically review your approach to compensation to identify where it may be driving the wrong behaviours.

- Think about how the belt buckle pipeline changes your approach to customer marketing and upsell processes.

9: Principle Six – Their choice, not yours

Much of what is done in the name of the customer is **done to** them, not at their request. Take two cornerstones of many customer success programmes: segmentation and customer journeys. You, the supplier, decide which segment they are in, usually based on spend. The segment they fall into then determines the customer journey they are allocated to. You decide the segment. You design and decide the journey they will follow. The customer is the recipient of your choices with no say in the process. Your choice; not theirs.

Let's start with understanding each of these two processes, as they relate to customer success.

- Segmentation is the act of aggregating customers into groups (or segments) with common needs as the basis for taking action.
- A customer journey is a series of interventions a customer takes to achieve their goals. These journeys are often broken down into detailed and scheduled sets of interventions.

In many B2B SaaS companies, the two processes are closely interlinked. Post-sale, most B2B SaaS companies allocate customers to a segment, which determines the intervention strategy – the journey(ies) – they receive. Before suggesting an alternative and, I think, better approach, let's explore the challenges in how segmentation and customer journeys are used by most B2B SaaS companies.

The problems with segmentation and customer journeys

Spend and need are not related

As I described in Chapter One, the predominant approach used by B2B SaaS companies allocates customers to one of three segments based on their revenue, or its more sophisticated sibling, potential revenue.

'High touch', 'medium touch' or 'tech touch' describes the approach to value delivery interventions allocated to these broad revenue buckets. Customers with the highest spend receive a high touch service whereas those with low spend levels are allocated to a self-service, technology-enabled service. This thinking is fundamentally flawed.

First, it assumes, wrongly in many cases, that all high-spending customers want a high-touch approach. Many don't. When Clicktools signed its first six figure ARR customer (at the time, our ACV was less than £10,000), we rushed to establish a personal, relationship-based success process with frequent contact with different stakeholders. The upshot? A highly dissatisfied customer: they said if we continued with that approach they would cancel. They told us they knew what they were doing and were actually quite busy! Their preference was to be left alone, for self-service wherever possible and the option of personal contact *when they wanted it*. Their spend bore no relationship to the sort of service we thought they wanted.

The mistake I made at Clicktools was to confuse my need to have that reassuring contact with what customers wanted. I have learned that this experience is not unique – other companies have had similar customer feedback as a result of placing their desire for customer contact ahead of what the customer really wanted. I believe personal relationships are important, but that does not equate to requiring, let alone mandating, high-touch or white glove service.

Preference for self-service

Research backs up an increasing preference for self-service. Nuance Enterprise[50] suggests that 67% of respondents prefer self-service over speaking to a company representative. BT futurologist Dr Nicola Millard writes that the phone is an important channel for people, even millennials: 47% start their search for help on an app but will pick up the phone if they have no success.[51] Note, they pick up the phone

---

[50] Quoted in https://www.zendesk.com/blog/searching-for-self-service/

because they can't get help via their first-choice media – the app. This is very different from choosing personal contact as a first choice. One factor driving the preference for self-service is speed of successful outcome. When asked what is important when an issue needs resolving by a company, 90% said speed of response and 88% said resolution at one touch.[52] Delivering against this expectation with a people-first approach is both expensive and not a preference for many.

The preference for self-service is growing but it is not new. History is replete with examples of self-service options being initially dismissed only for those naysayers being proved wrong as self-service becomes both the dominant and preferred method of consuming a service. Think ATMs in banking, self-service checkouts in shops (even before COVID-19) and self-service check-in kiosks at airports. Every time a self-serve option has been introduced, sceptics have dismissed it, usually to see it take hold and become the dominant service delivery method. Self-service plays to our psychological need to be in control, to do things when we want and not look silly if we don't know something. Companies that dismiss the desire for self-service suffer from a dangerous syndrome I call legacy thinking.

For naysayers, I have a simple request. Show me the evidence. Have you asked your customers if they prefer personal service over a **good** self-service first option? More importantly, have you tested the alternatives? Have you provided a well-designed self-service option and tested it alongside an equivalent personal service? I find that most are working from untested assumptions.

---

[51] https://soundcloud.com/mycustomer/what-will-customer-service-look-like-in-2030

[52] The real self-service economy. Professor Steven Van Bellegham. April 2013.

Confusing segmentation, service and affordability

Revenue-based approaches confuse segmentation, grouping customers to determine the service provided and affordability – managing the cost to serve. Proponents of this approach believe the cost of service should reflect customer revenue. Not for one minute am I suggesting that you should ignore the cost of delivering customer success. I believe customer success capabilities should make a significant contribution to margin – at the aggregate level. The error is to believe that spend has to reflect the revenue that specific customers generate: that spend is the primary determinant of service provided.

Based on revenue or potential revenue, companies design segment-specific journeys and use coverage analysis to determine the number of CSMs needed. It bears no relation to what customers want. This approach often drives margin deterioration by locking in costs that may be unnecessary. Crude, revenue-driven segmentation models force customers into your view of the world.

By the way, there is a subplot to the segmentation and service by spend approach. If revenue was a sound basis for segmentation (it isn't) then you should consider the spend of the cohort. 100 customers with an average ARR of £100,000 represents £10,000,000 ARR. 1,000 customers with an average ARR of £20,000 generates £20,000,000 ARR. If both groups had the same level of logo churn (say 10% annually) in which cohort should you invest your money and time to maximise retention?

You choose which customers you want to sell to, the value proposition offered and how much they pay. Customers acquired at lower price points still have a problem or opportunity to address. Not resolving that requirement will likely lead to churn, so if you are to recover CAC and generate an acceptable LTV:CAC ratio you have to develop a success process that delivers value to them at a cost you can afford. You can, of course, choose not to sell at lower price points, thus maintaining your ability to cost-effectively provide "high-touch" service where (if) that is an essential customer requirement.

Alternatively, you can consider a self-service first approach, lowering your overall cost to serve allowing you to generate an acceptable return at lower price points and even greater margin at higher price points.

Journeys don't reflect reality

The concept of journey mapping originated in the B2C world, where the focus is on the individual. In a B2B context, they seek to describe the challenges and work a customer does and how, therefore, you can help the customer. The problems with customer journeys arise because of the chasm between the journey a supplier describes and the reality of people's working lives. Every detailed customer journey I have seen is a vague approximation of reality and therefore poses as many risks as it does solutions. There are a number of reasons for this.

Commenting on the process of building customer journeys, CS community leader Jay Nathansaid, *"You can't map out 100 different customer journeys cos that would be customisation, so we focus on the 1 or 2 most impactful."* [53] Nathan recognises that to deliver the detail needed to drive a series of interventions is an impossible task. Even if you could describe complete journeys, customers are not linear or rational and are unlikely to follow them. They are, rightly, focused on their work, their goals, their journey. Change will only be successful if the two journeys exactly coincide. What happens when the customer's goals and priorities change? Building the rules to accommodate every permutation of change is mission impossible.

Atomisation of the buyer requires a deep understanding of the specific roles people play. It is no longer enough to map a "customer journey". You need to understand the current motivations, challenges and priorities of each individual you deal with. Capturing all those nuances and alternatives in a journey map is challenging beyond belief. The maps I have seen, even the best, lack the personal context, depth and irrationality that is inherent in most customers' relationships and

---

[53] Quoted in the podcast Creating CS, Episode 14. March 2020.

interactions. If building something truly representative is not possible, then why bother at all?

I think customer journeys have limited benefit for the work companies put into them. They are very useful in one context only: as part of a high-level view of how the organisation works; one element of the holistic approach to organisation design discussed in the previous chapter.

Sophistication is not uniform

My experience is that those buying smaller packages at lower price points often need more help because they are just stepping into that domain – testing the water – and therefore less sophisticated. That applies to individuals and teams in larger companies as well as smaller companies. Even the most sophisticated companies and individuals have areas where skills and knowledge are weaker in certain areas. They are going to need more hand-holding in some activities and will want to be left alone in others where their competence and confidence are high. Driving people through a fixed journey based on spend is, therefore, sorely mistaken and definitely not descriptive of a customer-focused organisation.

Providing the appropriate level of service requires a far deeper understanding of the roles than I have ever seen in any customer journey. The segment is determined by data that identify an intersection of:

- The challenges and priorities facing the individual;

- The individual's sophistication in the task in hand;

- Their preference for consuming help and advice.

In essence, you need a much more dynamic, data-driven approach to segmentation that also embraces individual choice. Given these fundamental problems, how should we approach segmentation and customer journeys? My answer is scrap them both and replace them with context-driven Next Best Value.

Next Best Value: Dynamic segmentation and journeys

Next Best Value is a derivative of next best offer, a technique which originated in B2C marketing. This value-focused application of the approach is more sophisticated and generates contextually richer interventions than defined customer journeys. It recognises that there are many paths to the customer's end goal and that the path is dynamic not pre-determined, responding to changes in an individual's behaviour and preference. Like Value Elements, an NBV is granular and independent of other actions.

Here's how NBV works.

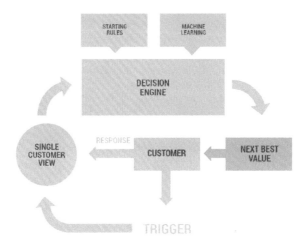

Fig 9.1: Next Best Value engine

A trigger – something the individual does (including doing nothing) updates their record, creating an updated context. The heart of the system is the decision engine, which combines data from the single customer view with rules to determine the best value element for that individual at that point in time. This is presented to the customer, and the action they take and its outcome (response) updates the single customer view. The cycle begins again. This repeating cycle crafts a customer journey which is contextually rich, dynamic and unique to that individual.

The rules may be set manually initially, but as the engine progresses, the real power lies in the application of machine learning to identify relationships between actions and successful outcomes. The result is a blend of manual and machine generated rules tuned to maximise the likelihood of success.

Each NBV relates to a Value Element and sets out what, why and how. "What" is a description of the action (or series of actions) needed. "Why" explains the rationale: why the individual should take the action – the benefits it generates. "How" contains the resources provided to help the individual complete the action.

Isn't NBV just a series of interactions within a customer journey, I hear you say? Well they are interactions but the big difference is the underlying assumption. The vast majority of customer journeys I have seen are linear; C follows A and B. Some of the more sophisticated journeys include (a limited number of) alternative paths, but linearity remains the underlying design principle. Unfortunately, real life is rarely so linear or predictable; it's chaotic, repetitive, even random. Students of military doctrine will be familiar with the quote *"No plan of operations reaches with any certainty beyond the first encounter with the enemy's main force."* [54] I think the same is true of the journeys you try to get your customers to follow. They're not trying to fight you; they just want to get on with their job, their way.

The linearity of customer journeys does not reflect the messy lives your customers live. All too often, customer journeys lock people into a path that does not reflect their specific needs. NBV uses data to identify the current context of the individual and suggest what they should do next. There is no assumption of linearity: context drives content. Any similarity in the path taken by two people with the same

[54] Attributed to Prussian Army Chief of Staff Graf Helmuth Karl Bernhard von Moltke, 1880

role is entirely a function of their context. NBVs provide a much more dynamic "sense and respond" approach that seeks to nudge customers to their next value threshold rather than dictate what they should do.

Implementing Next Best Value

There are three keys to implementing an approach based on NBV.

Single customer view

Today, B2B SaaS companies have access to a plethora of data about their customers, although (foolishly in my mind) many do not invest in building a rich single customer view. Product, sentiment, transaction, preference, role, relationship and goal data are relatively easy to collate. These data provide a much richer context of the customer than ever before, and herein lies the key. Combining this rich customer view with real-time execution systems enables the delivery of contextually rich, highly personalised experiences. Mass customisation of experiences may not be simple but is now achievable for those with the will. A rich, single view of the customer is the foundation. Single customer view does not mean a single database or system. Rather, it is a commitment across the organisation to ensure data in different systems are compatible and able to be integrated.

Robust, self-learning systems

NBV is, in large part, a technology play: to attempt it without technology will lead to failure. NBV is a repetitive cycle of data analysis and action. The number of data points involved makes the number crunching too much for any individual and that is before applying rules to prioritise alternative NBVs. As a minimum, the underlying algorithm has to consider the following data points:

- Previous actions/interventions;
- Goals for a given use case;
- Value Elements: achieved and current;
- Product usage;
- Sentiment;

- Channel preferences;
- Propensity to act;
- Sophistication.

The power of NBV to deliver contextually rich interventions is amped up by exploiting the power of machine learning and predictive analytics. Machine learning's capability to uncover the causal correlations between patterns of activity and successful results is already being used by some CS operations. The field of value analytics will grow significantly as the underlying technologies develop further.

Library of Value Elements

There's no point in having the greatest data and technology if you don't have anything to harness to them, and that's where Value Elements re-enter the play. Remember, Value Elements are about delivering small, role-specific, measurable packets of value; an approach which lends itself to being embedded into your product. Whilst product is the primary vehicle for presenting the content, it does not have to be the only channel. The same content can be used in person-to-person interactions or via communities.

Value Elements can comprise content of many kinds, for example:

- Product walk-throughs;
- Configuration guides;
- Videos, talk-throughs, written guides;
- Best practice case studies;
- Workbooks;
- Quizzes/tests.

You will need to track consumption of the different Value Elements. This will enable progress reporting and, more importantly, help you to understand the relationships between different Value Elements consumed and measurable value achieved. This learning will help refine the advice and guidance you provide to the different roles served.

Advice to CEOs

- What they spend does not determine the service they want.
- It sounds obvious, but it's all about taking the customer's perspective. Don't ask them what they want; ask them about their challenges, and ask them regularly. Use those insights to drive innovation in product and value enablement.
- Think about how you can be persuasive not prescriptive when helping customers achieve their goals.
- It's never too early to be thinking about building your single view of the customer. Understanding context is the basis of Next Best Value.

10: Principle Seven – Code scales better than people

The purpose of a B2B SaaS company is to communicate and deliver value to its chosen customers; ergo, the product must be the primary vehicle for delivering it. One of the old ten laws of customer success states "Product is your only scalable differentiator". Despite this, very few B2B SaaS products have a meaningful value enablement (customer success) process embedded in them.

Customers buy your product to address a need, to resolve a pain or a gain. Fulfilment of this need, value delivery, is the primary driver of renewal and expansion revenues. If you are like most CEOs, you address this challenge by building a customer success team. After all, everyone tells you this is best practice. I know because I was founder and CEO at a successful SaaS company that did just that. But what if I, and you, could do better?

Looking back, I was wrong. I now believe there is a way to deliver the same or better value for customers at significantly lower cost whilst maintaining, or better still, improving customer satisfaction. What if you could deliver these results with a strategy that truly scales and delivers higher margins? What if there was an approach that drives increased valuations? This is the promise of product-enabled (product-led) value. The idea is not new, although it has taken on greater impetus with the growth of the product-led growth business model.

Rationale for product-enabled value

I have been extolling the concept of product-enabled value[55] for B2B SaaS companies for several years, for reasons I will explain. I am now

---

[55] I have shifted from using the term product-led customer success to product-enabled value. This is because too many companies confuse a customer success team with customer value as a company-wide approach. Using the word "enabled" recognises the

of the view that it is a natural and unstoppable movement for the following four reasons.

Core to purpose

Embedding the delivery of value, the customer success process, in the product is at the core of the two fundamental elements of a B2B SaaS company.

First, B2B SaaS companies are product companies. You chose to build a product company, not a consultancy. You may have made this choice because you know that the valuation multiples of recurring product revenue are significantly higher than service revenues. You may be an engineer and just know how you can solve a need in a novel way. Whatever the reason, you chose to build a product. Second, as CEO of a B2B SaaS company, you know that your success, repeatable and scalable growth, is founded on your customers being successful. If they don't get the value they are seeking, you are much less likely to get the renewal and expansion revenue that drives NRR, CLTV and the CLTV:CAC ratio.

Product-enabled value is a vehicle to address these two core elements simultaneously.

Natural trend of automation

The history of technology teaches us three things. First, technology will always advance and deliver new capabilities. Second, those new technologies will make some jobs redundant and create new jobs. Third, attempts to resist the changes are futile.

Mechanisation drove the industrial revolution and replaced whole swathes of manual jobs with a new kind of work: tending machines. As mechanisation advanced, more complex products succumbed. Information technology did the same for low level administrative tasks

emphasis on supporting individual choice over prescriptive success.

in the 1950s and is now climbing the added-value ladder. AI is turbo-charging that push into areas that were previously considered impossible to automate. A report[56] by The Brookings Institute into AI's impact on jobs found that *"Better-paid, white-collar occupations may be most exposed to AI"* and *"Business-finance-tech industries will be more exposed"*. As tech entrepreneur and investor Marc Andreessen said,[57] *"In short, software is eating the world."* Customer success is not exempt.

It's what many customers want

I have made this point many times but many still reject it. Customers increasingly want an effective self-service approach as their first choice. The history of self-service shows that to be the case. Many of the naysayers hold on to this legacy mindset, blaming other things, but as Pogo says,[58] *"We have met the enemy: it is us."*

Many have failed to build well-designed, easy-to-use products. They hide this failure behind the "our product is complicated" excuse. Many products solve difficult problems and/or multiple customer challenges. That does not mean large chunks of the process of helping the customer achieve value cannot be understood and codified. Some cannot or don't want to challenge their existing approach and business model, unwilling to tackle the difficult choices such a change involves. Some project their beliefs and ideals onto customers; others question why change something that works. All may have some validity save one thing: many customers want a self-serve option as their first choice.

---

[56] "What jobs are affected by AI? Better-paid, better-educated workers face the most exposure" Brookings Institute Nov 2019

[57] https://genius.com/Marc-andreessen-why-software-is-eating-the-world-annotated

[58] Walt Kelly first used the quote on a poster for Earth Day in 1970.

It makes sense financially

Whilst a higher purpose may be fundamental to what drives you, you probably have an interest in the value of your company. Even if you aren't bothered about valuations, your investors definitely are. Money matters.

I experienced first-hand the valuation impact of product-enabled value delivery in 2010 with a call asking if I'd be interested in meeting Dave Goldberg, the CEO of Survey Monkey. When the CEO of the gorilla in your market (pun intended) asks to meet, you jump on a plane. They wanted to acquire a stake in Clicktools, and as the conversation progressed, we got to the meat: how much they would pay for a 49.9% stake. We stated our case for a certain revenue multiple based on our track record and a rich business model underpinning a realistic understanding of what we could achieve. Dave accepted this, then added the "yes but"; there's always a "yes but". In this case there were two "yes buts". The first was our services revenue (about 12%), which he valued less because it carried a lower margin and was only scalable linearly. The second was two items in our P&L that, whilst necessary, were in his opinion too high: customer support and customer success. Dave's argument was that a better product experience could significantly reduce these, enabling us to scale with a better margin and therefore warrant a higher valuation. We did the deal but it cost me! The lesson stuck and set me off on a path to product-enabled value delivery.

This financial impact derives from three factors:

Code scales better than people. Code scales logarithmically; people linearly. With people-first customer success, logo growth requires a proportional increase in people. Productivity improvements will improve margins, but this will be incremental. Code, on the other hand, has an initial build cost, but growth in customer numbers does not proportionally increase costs. Both models incur costs of maintenance, and here, the people approach has the edge initially as people are great at figuring things out on the move. Once the changes have been designed, again code scales better. I have modelled the scale impact and the code approach incurs an initial financial hit as the solution is built but thereafter drives significantly greater returns.

Value drives upsells. Chapter Eight: Success is selling, recognises the close link between the value that customers achieve and the growth of your revenue. Product-enabled value is based on a deep understanding of the actions needed to achieve value. Bringing actions and outcomes together underpins understanding of causal correlations. This allows you to present value-based upsell messaging: "Want this? Buy this!" Delivering this in-app has two advantages:

- The opportunity is presented in a rich context specific to the user role, their goals and the time they need it. The richer the context, the higher the buying propensity.
- It scales at margin. Even if there is subsequent intervention from people, the initial opportunity is created and, to a large degree, extremely well qualified. It is, in the language of product-led-growth, a PQL: a product-qualified lead.

Faster, data-driven learning curves. App telemetry and user path monitoring are staples of any B2B SaaS business. Bringing value activities and achievements into this dataset enriches the understanding between activity and customer value and enables A-B testing of value delivery interventions, thereby speeding up the learning curve. Faster, more effective learning strengthens the understanding of and thereby improves the value delivery process. Delivering more value for customers faster and easier is a recipe for growth through improved retention, expansion and advocacy.

Product-enabled, not product only

Advocating for a product-enabled approach is not the same as saying product should be the only available channel for delivering value to customers. Many of the leaders in product-led acquisition operate hybrid models, backing up product-led with more traditional inside-sales and account management capabilities. The same is required for product-enabled value. I believe great value enablement leads with product but also makes it very easy for customers to get extra help through different channels when **they** need it.

Some companies intentionally design a hybrid model. Email provider Superhuman requires a person-to-person onboarding session, most of which is not about using the product but about developing strategies for managing email to suit the user's needs. This leads to greater success for both the customer and the company – they know because they measure both.

Designing a product-enabled value process must include a "help me!" option at each step with access to additional resources and a fail-safe, speak to us option. The key is to use data and customer feedback to continually chip away at the need for human intervention. This approach is used extensively in customer support and is known as call-deflection. The book *The Best Service is No Service*[59] sets out eight principles as the basis of a manifesto: *"Stop coping with customer demand for service, which simply increase customers' frustration; instead challenge customer demand for service, so that, ideally, everything works perfectly, eliminating defects and confusion so that there is no need at all for customers, or prospective customers, to contact the company for information or for help."* Read that manifesto again. It should guide your company's approach to delivering customer success.

One of the adherents of this manifesto is Amazon, the company with the mission "to be the Earth's most customer-centric company" and with world class levels of growth, profitability AND customer satisfaction. Great self-service starts with the needs of your chosen customers; the financial benefits are just a significant, added benefit.

The sceptics will point out that Amazon is a consumer business. Yes, and increasingly, consumer businesses are the model B2B should follow. I came to understand that Survey Monkey had grown up with a consumer mindset, selling mainly to individuals. It entered the

---

[59] The Best Service is no Service. Bill Price and David Jaffe. ISBN 978-0-470-18908-5

enterprise space knowing how to address a real need with a self-service, product-led first approach. This consumer (think user, individual) approach is increasingly preferred by B2B customers. In his remarks to investors in Feb 2021, HubSpot CEO Brian Halligan said,[60] *"The way people want to buy is changing. And, increasingly, they want a very light touch experience. And, increasingly, they want parts of their products and maybe all of their products even on the B2B side to be some sort of an e-commerce [touch] transaction."* It's not just how they want to buy; it's how they want to interact with the company across the lifecycle, including how you help them achieve value.

A brief detour

Before delving further into how to productise value delivery, I want to take a short detour to explore a major issue with how most companies build their success or value enablement processes. A friend of mine talks about three types of change. "Change-to" is directive: do this. "Change-with" is consensual: we are going this way and here's why you should come along. "Change-by" is intrinsic: I choose. Whilst each have their role, change-by is most likely to be successful. The problem is most success plans follow the "change-to" approach. Suppliers dictate the actions, the order those actions should be done and how they should be done. They smack of a parent–child relationship, no pun intended. In the context of success plans, change-by means giving customers choice of what they want to do and supporting them as a coach. It's success on the customer's terms, not yours. I think this is fundamental to the future of customer success and particularly product-enabled value.

---

[60] HubSpot, Inc. (HUBS) CEO Brian Halligan on Q4 2020 Results - Earnings Call Transcript

seekingalpha.com/article/4405513-HubSpot-inc-hubs-ceo-brian-halligan-on-q4-2020-results-earnings-call-transcript?mail_subject=hubs-...

My vision of product-enabled value

What follows is a personal vision of product-enabled value. There is no company I am aware of that has built all this capability, although parts of it exist. I am, however, aware of a number of companies working on implementing comprehensive product-enabled value processes.

There are six actions involved in product-enabled value.[61] These actions do not imply a linear process: each action is essentially independent. There may be some dependencies, especially in the setup phase. Dependencies that are absolutely essential should be embedded in Value Elements. This unstructured approach breaks away from the "we-tell, you-do" method most companies use when building customer value processes.

Discovery

Value enablement starts with understanding the key determinants of how the individual will use your product: their role and the pain/gain they choose to work on. These will give a steer on the issues/capabilities to be addressed and the value metrics of interest. The two will also guide a conversation about the product features of importance. Productivity tool Notion captures this information in just a couple of simple screens.

---

[61] The actions are not different from those required for any form of value delivery. Productising them does, however, call for greater clarity.

Fig 9.2: Notion online discovery (copyright Notion Labs Inc)

Note that Notion reflect the roles and uses (pain/gains) they most commonly serve, and they keep it simple. Companies that use traditional acquisition will often capture some of this information in the sales process and it should therefore be piped-in. Free trials and freemium offerings have an edge here as they blur the boundary between selling and value enablement.

Start

The sooner you get the customer using your product and seeing value, the better. The next step, therefore, is to get the customer to select an area to work on and get started! Most success plans set out a fixed order that customers are instructed to follow: the parent–child approach. I believe it preferable to give control to the individual. This transfer of power involves providing customers with the means to make informed choices, because choice and commitment go hand-in-hand. Paradoxically, people often get anxious when given too much choice. Our friend psychology comes to our aid with the Influence of Options. Rather than set out a fixed path or a multitude of choices,

121

present options where choices are beneficial. "Save time by using one of our templates" or "Build a plan to suit your specific needs." A few options with clear benefits gives the individual control without stress. One of those options should be to bypass the success process completely and just start using the product.

Set a goal

Once the person has selected an area to work on, you should help them set **their** first goal. This goal should be set to deliver a meaningful but achievable improvement in something that matters to **them**: a level of performance that shows meaningful progress. Note my emphasis on the individual and not some nebulous concept of outcome that is removed from their work. Which goals to set is driven by the value metrics and business impact content in the Value Framework, which includes a role specific perspective of the data.

The sophistication of goal setting is dependent on the quality of data available. At its simplest, it is capturing a value for current performance and then upscaling it. At the other end of scale, companies are using value analytics to propose a goal. Imagine a level of customer understanding where the dialogue goes as follows: "People in your role and experience in companies like yours typically achieve a median performance of X and a stretch goal of Y. What goal do you want to aim for?"

Advise and guide

With pain/gain and goal established, the work of helping the individual achieve their goal begins. Enter Value Elements. Value Elements contain the advice and guidance to help people address the pain/gain they have chosen to work on. Remember, Value Elements focus on small, incremental improvements, leveraging concepts of psychology such as hyperbolic discounting bias and the subadditivity effect.

I think of Value Elements as playing cards, each describing the "What, Why and How" for a required solution. The number of Value Elements will differ according to the complexity of a given pain/gain. This is also an area where dependencies may be required: stick to the absolute minimum and leave the user as much freedom of choice as possible. Users should be able to select the cards, the Value Elements they want into their working area, thereby creating their own, personalised success plans. Their choice – not yours.

There will of course be customers that are less sophisticated or just prefer an easy life. This is where template plans come into play. Rather than select and build their own plan, a user can select a pre-built plan built to match (as closely as possible) their role, sophistication and other criteria, e.g. industry sector. Future plan builders will use machine learning and artificial intelligence to suggest the Next Best Value Element, explaining the relationship between certain activity patterns and high performing customers.

Iterate

An approach to success plans based on a singular outcome typically has all the steps mapped out. The journey is essentially fixed: a reductionist approach that assumes one right way. A product-enabled approach enables an iterative, user-driven approach. I see this as the difference between coaching and teaching paradigms. The coaching approach is about helping the individual understand and choose options and providing support to achieve them, whereas the teaching approach is didactic.

In addition to playing to the psychology of small steps, an iterative approach demonstrates your commitment to continually delivering value to the people you serve. Interactions focus on helping them achieve that next value; pointless check-ins are eliminated as customers are continually presented with content specific to goals and challenges they have chosen.

Provide feedback

The final element of product-enabled value is feedback of two types: activity progress and value attainment.

Value dashboards, specific to each user, show the pain/gain points they have addressed and progress in those currently active. They also display changes over time in the value metrics that matter to them and, where appropriate, measures of business impact. Value dashboards replace much of what traditional CS presents as part of quarterly business reviews with continuous reporting of value achieved. This timely, context -rich and in-product feedback is a continual reminder of measurable achievement; a reinforcement of the case for continued and possibly expanded use of your product. It is a continuing validation of the decision to buy and reinforcement of the case to continue using. It is also a means to enhance learning. Rapid, repeated cycles create more opportunities for learning, performance improvement and more course corrections. In today's world, speed is often a source of advantage.

Many decision makers and influencers involved with the purchase of your product will not be users, but ensuring they are aware of the value your product is providing is essential to renewal and expansion opportunities. Product-enabled customer success needs, therefore, to include ways to reach these non-users. That might be as simple as a periodic email of key results or more sophisticated integration into core business and performance management tools.

New tools and approaches

Central to product-enabled value is a shared space where people from the customer and supplier sides can work together. It is a space where the six actions described above are enacted. Using the portal, customers can select the Value Elements they want to work on, set goals, track their activities and progress and help each other.

Whilst collaboration tools are not new, value delivery specific portals are new to the market. Tools like MetaCX go beyond a space to share documents and converse by providing tools to build value delivery processes. MetaCX calls their portals "bridges": a shared space where two or more parties can build and collaborate around success plans, including the ability to embed the process into your application. Rather than focusing on measuring and managing value delivery teams, these products put the creation and measurement of value itself centre-stage.

I have suggested that B2B apps will become more like consumer-oriented products. One area where consumer products outperform most of their B2B counterparts is in usability, and one field specifically leads the pack: gaming apps. I think there is much to learn from how developers build games; an approach mastered by serial B2B entrepreneur Rahul Vohra. People choose to play games: they do so because they want to, not because they must. Vohra applies game theory (not its much simpler cousin gamification) when building his email app Superhuman.[62] Vohra describes five principles of game design that he applies to building B2B apps:

- The user must always know what to do next;
- The user must always know how to do it;
- The user must be free from other distractions;
- The product should always provide clear and immediate feedback;
- The product should balance challenge and skill: not too easy (boredom); not too hard (anxiety).

This quintet forms a great guide to building product-enabled value, although I would add one more:

- The product should be fun to use.

Business is serious, but that does not mean it cannot involve fun. Fun is engaging; fun is productive; fun is enjoyable: all of which are important for effective products, personal development and motivation.

---

[62] For Rahul's full explanation:
https://a16z.com/2020/01/13/game-design-not-gamification/

New capabilities

Product-enabled value will change the work and capabilities your company needs compared with traditional customer success organisations; changes that are already underway in more sophisticated B2B SaaS companies.

CS as product owner

In a performant B2B SaaS company, revenue from existing customers soon exceeds new logo sales. That, and the focus of product as the delivery vehicle for customer success, places product front and centre of delivering customer value. It is natural, then, that CS is a locus for the agile product ownership role. I also believe that product and development know-how will become an essential attribute of a CS leader. Intelliflo, a UK-based provider of SaaS for financial advisors, brings customer success and product under a Chief Operating Officer role and delivers great results.

Value researcher

Understanding individuals, their goals and challenges is a requirement of any effective organisation but one that few companies resource effectively. Product-enabled value is founded on a deep understanding of the customer; an understanding captured in a Value Framework (described above). Winners will understand their chosen customers better than the competition. This is not a one-off exercise: companies will need to maintain their Value Frameworks.

Value content manager

Short, practical content contextually presented via the product is an essential part of product-enabled value. Creating and maintaining this content requires full time resource. Relying on marketing to do this will not suffice: their focus is typically on acquisition, and value enablement content is a different beast, although some of the skillsets, for example copy writing, are common to both.

Value advisors

An increasingly productised value delivery process will remove much of what traditional CSMs and professional service consultants currently do. The two roles will merge and focus on higher level activities. Key will be helping customers with the psychology and management of change. The skillset will be more akin to a business consultant, with a salary to match.

What becomes of the CS department?

These capabilities are not necessarily discrete jobs, particularly in the early stages. Nor are they capabilities that form part of the responsibilities of a CS department. They are just as likely to be part of existing roles in product marketing rather than customer success. Where they sit is less important than what they do and how they work and influence across the organisation.

So what becomes of the traditional CS organisation in a world where customer value shapes every aspect of the customer lifecycle? It will continue as a discrete department. Remember, product-enabled does not mean product only. Customers will continue to need personal contact to solve unique or more complex challenges that are, initially at least, difficult to codify. Delivering value also goes beyond the use of the product: changes to processes, metrics and skills are often needed. Whilst content can be provided through the product to help this, the challenges of driving change are around motivation and confidence as much as know-how. These challenges are where people excel and will perform better than even the very best AI for many years to come.

The CS department will continue, but the work will shift. Manual interventions will become fewer as more are productised. They will require different skills with a greater emphasis on guiding personal change replacing product and process interventions. Paradoxically, the growth of product-enabled value will strengthen the need for customer coaching skills. The shift to product-enabled value will also see an acceleration in the growth and integration of enablement roles. Revenue operations will become value enablement.

What the future holds

I have no doubt that more value delivery focused apps will appear over the next few years. Their real impact, however, will be in strengthening the importance and focus of the value delivery process. Led by the open-source movement, I foresee the creation of libraries of value delivery routines that companies can build into their products, much as they now do with AI and ML capabilities. Perhaps Amazon Web Services, Google Cloud and Microsoft Azure will become the leading suppliers of CS software.

In the same vein, entrepreneurial specialists will codify their experience and ideas and build and sell Value Elements. Whilst these might start as being company/application specific, I can envisage a market for Value Elements: an e-Bay for value. Such a market will drive down the costs and development time needed to build product-enabled value capabilities.

Looking further ahead, I believe we will see companies that productise value delivery gain a further advantage by leading the introduction of performance-based pricing models. Their data-driven insights into what it takes to deliver measurable value for individuals will enable them to price based on value delivered. Imagine being able to say to customers: based on our understanding of this domain and your current performance, we promise you a return of X. For this, you pay Y, and if we deliver 2X, you pay 1.5Y.

Is this possible without embedding the value delivery process in your product? Yes, but I believe less effectively. It brings together the work your product does, data-driven goal setting, contextually rich guidance and the power of immediate feedback. It simplifies the challenge of integrating activity and value data enabling deeper insights.

And after all, delivering value is the raison d'être of your business; the reason you built a product.

Advice to CEOs

- Productising the value enablement process is key to scaling, core to the purpose of a product business and great for valuations.
- Building a deep understanding of value and how to measure it is an essential foundation. Give it the resources it needs. You can't productise what you don't understand.
- Think about converting your best CSM into a product manager to drive this.
- Make fun and enjoyment a design principle for productising value delivery, and leverage psychology to encourage adoption and sustain involvement.
- Recognise that you will have to invest in building out and maintain the content need to enact Value Elements.

PART THREE

From ideas to action

Where I try to wrap it all up in a way that will help you bring the principles to life.

11: From idea to action

The seven principles are the foundation stones of a customer focused B2B SaaS company, but where do you start? In this final chapter, I will share ideas to help bring the principles to life.

Focus on three core frameworks

The seven principles describe key elements of a customer focused B2B SaaS company. The most effective way to bring these principles to life is to focus on three core frameworks and how they work together. The three are:

1. Your Ideal Customer Profile, describing both the types of companies you target and, more importantly, the people (key roles) you sell to and serve (Chapter Six);

2. The Value Framework that encapsulates a deep understanding of the challenges facing the key roles and how you communicate and enable value through the messaging, products, services and guidance you provide (Chapter Seven);

3. The Customer Engagement Blueprint, the overall architecture that shapes the processes your specialists build (Chapter Five).

Individually, each of these frameworks are of great value. Together they are hugely powerful, as each enhances and reinforces the other forming a rich and deeply coherent vision for how your organisation works. The ICP, particularly the Role Profile, describes the challenges each key role faces. Marketing, sales, product and value enablement each develop content for the different stages of the Customer Engagement Blueprint, using the Value Framework to shape coherent messaging and processes.

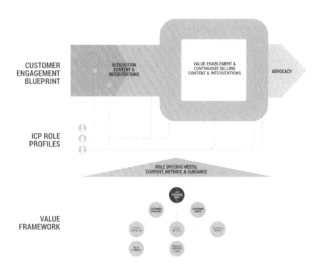

Fig 11.1 Core framework integration

This is not a one-off exercise: nor is it a programme to develop a single, detailed, all-singing and dancing customer journey. Resist the temptation of the reductionist approach. You will spend an inordinate amount of time building a map that has little practical value and will be out of date in days. Your job is to ensure the three frameworks are developed collaboratively, understood across the company and used as touchstones for the myriad of actions and initiatives that enact them. Use them as structures that shape content and processes, as a taxonomy for resources and as a means to build understanding of customers. You should provide means for people across the company to contribute to their maintenance. Crowdsourcing builds engagement, deeper understanding and richer content. These frameworks provide a reference point for specialists to contribute their expertise in a way that maintains coherence without being directive.

Remember also the vital role played by metrics and compensation plans in shaping collaboration and culture. Focus on metrics that show how the organisation as a whole is performing.

Curate your data

Did you ever do dot-to-dot puzzles as a kid? Do you remember how the more complicated puzzles, the ones with many dots, generated a richer picture? Now imagine the challenge of discerning the picture if the dots are on different pages or in different books. This illustrates the power of data strategy to drive insights: the more data points you have, the richer the insights you can generate. Your data strategy must ensure you can always join the dots.

Data is a cornerstone of delivering iterative value and continuous selling. Understanding context: the ability to use data to help to understand the individual's current situation and identifying patterns of activities that correlate measurable improvements in value metrics both rely on your ability to master data. These capabilities underpin a Next Best Value engine. The ability to quickly and easily bring together different types of data to drive contextually rich interventions, test hypotheses and identify causal correlations demands data integration. This must span data of many types: customer (e.g. role, intention, sentiment), detailed product usage, transactional, value achievement and financial.

When I formed Clicktools in 2000, we adopted the free version of Salesforce, going on to becoming a paying customer. As we grew, we built out almost all our functionality in this one app; we had to, there was little else on the market. We built an integration that pulled in key product usage data, crafted our health scoring and used the integration with our own feedback product to feed-in form and survey data. The lack of alternatives serendipitously helped us build a single customer view. As we grew, I resisted pressures to buy point solutions and insisted that any software we might adopt had to have a rich integration with Salesforce. I selected Financial Force to replace a legacy accounting solution because it was built on the Salesforce platform, giving us the ability to easily view, report on and test hypotheses that spanned customer, operational and financial data. Reporting, including board reporting, was all driven by Salesforce dashboards, saving time, minimising errors and removing the "whose data is right" arguments that come from disconnected datasets. The biggest benefit came from the ability for anyone to rapidly test their own hypotheses. Short learning cycles are vital in a SaaS business where retention and growth are often the result of many small improvements.

The SaaS application ecosystem is very different today, with an app for everything and powerful data integration technologies, so I am not suggesting you build it all in Salesforce. I do, however, urge you to think deeply about the data structures you need to build and exploit coherence in your data. Always ask how the data generated by new apps will be integrated to enhance your ability to drive insights and test hypotheses. Ensure people understand the power of good data and provide them with the tools, skills and motivation to use data to support their work and decisions. Be obsessed about your company's ability to exploit data. Remember your dot-to-dot puzzles and understand that the more data you have, the more intuitive you become.

Build customer and financial literacy

The core tenet of this book is that value to customers drives financial performance and, therefore, the valuation of your business. The two key components are customer and financial literacy, where literacy is the ability to understand and use knowledge of the two domains. An important driver of the quality of decisions is understanding context. Customers, financial performance and how each relates to the other are an important part of that context. The more people understand this relationship, the better decisions they will make.

Customer literacy

You cannot build a customer-focused organisation if people in your organisation don't understand your customers. At the simplest level, building customer literacy means helping people understand the characteristics of the three core frameworks (see above).

Socialising the frameworks is, therefore, the first level of understanding you need to build. This will have started with broad involvement in their development, but that franchise has to be extended to the whole organisation. Everyone should be able to describe the key characteristics of the companies and people you serve (ICP), their challenges (Value Framework) and the way you communicate and deliver value across the lifecycle (Customer Engagement Blueprint). And I do mean everyone, although I recognise that some will need a more detailed understanding than others.

First level customer literacy shares what has been developed, but as we all know, customer needs change, many of which will need a response from your company. Addressing this dynamic represents the second level of customer literacy. This centres around how you teach people to listen for, capture and validate the changing needs of customers then translate them into new areas and ways to deliver value. Teaching people how to ask questions[63] that uncover real needs is key to this. Curating this crowd-sourced information calls on the capabilities of the value researcher and value content manager roles discussed in Chapter Ten.

Financial literacy

Numbers tell an important part of the story, so if people are to understand your company's narrative, they have to understand its financial performance. Building financial literacy will be rewarded with better decisions. It pushes people to think about how their ideas and decisions will impact the business as well as benefit customers. Sharing financial performance will have greater impact if people understand the numbers. The better they understand company performance, the better able they are to understand and make decisions. On sharing financial data, I would advise you share more, rather than less; even bad news. You have employed adults and they can deal with bad as well as good news. In fact, if you don't share bad news, you cannot blame people for taking actions that don't help. That's your failure, not theirs.

---

[63] The Mom Test (ibid)

What should you teach them? Here's a suggested curriculum:

- How a B2B SaaS company is valued;
- The structure of a B2B SaaS P&L;
- The key metrics used to track your business: what and why;
- The impact of different approaches on acquisition, retention and expansion costs;
- The financial model of your pipeline and the wider business;
- Productivity strategies and how they impact profitability.

Personal and career development is another benefit of building financial literacy. As people take on more senior roles, financial literacy is an increasingly important competence. Start their development early.

How the two interact

Given the scarcity of both cash and time, many of the decisions your organisation faces are about choosing which of several good options to invest in. Building customer and financial literacy helps this decision-making process by better equipping people to assess benefits for both customers and the company. Making decisions on only one dimension often leads to sub-optimal use of scarce resources. Push people to find solutions that deliver on both dimensions. This is what I call seeking "and" answers; this and that, not this or that. Avoiding the trade-off trap requires people to build a deeper understanding of the problem and be more creative and thereby leads to better solutions.

One simple approach is to teach your people to rank proposals by impact on value achieved for customers and financial impact on the business. For example, a product enhancement may be ranked by the quantum of value it enables for target customers (value x customer count) and by cost to deliver. Candidates for action are those that deliver the biggest value quantum with the lowest resources. I want to stress that this is a guide to aid decision making, not a substitute for it.

You can encourage this. Always ask how this will help customers and the business; help them build models that test the financial implications of their ideas and decisions.

Lead with vision and values

Success by design starts with vision and values. In *Organising for the new normal,*[64] Professor Constantinos Markides talks about how to create autonomy without losing control. Markides highlights two key parameters, strategy and values, which create the canvas onto which everyone across the organisation can paint. I prefer vision (not strategy) and values, but the premise is the same: if you have hired great people your role is to give them the canvas, provide the right tools and information then get out of their way.

The canvas is a sketch describing your overall vision, your company's values and the core of the three frameworks. I use the word "sketch" purposefully. It intentionally implies a lack of detail and a visual representation. Its purpose is to set broad boundaries within which people have freedom to innovate, decide and act. The more detail you include, the more you constrain people's ability to contribute. Your work is to drive conversations across the organisation that require people to question, interpret and challenge elements of the canvas then act in accordance with their understanding of it. You will disagree with some of the decisions and actions people take. You will be tempted to use your position, experience and authority to over-rule. Before you do, try these techniques that I have learned from two highly respected business leaders.

Bill Gore, of GoreTex fame, talked about decision making using the metaphor of a ship's Plimsoll line,[65] the markings that determine

---

[64] "Organising for the new normal: Prepare your company for the journey of continuous disruption" Constantinos C Markides. ISBN 978-1398600799

[65] Gore shared this at a conference for CEOs I attended.

where ships float given different loads. Gore was comfortable with people making decisions that were above the Plimsoll line: they might make the ship slower or less attractive, but they won't sink the ship. He explained the importance of wide consultation, debate and escalation for actions that require change below the waterline. Gore said an important role of the CEO is to determine where the company's Plimsoll line is drawn. He added that, unfortunately, many CEOs draw their Plimsoll line just below the top of the funnel!

Jeff Bezos recognises the need for consultation on key decisions; the result of which he does not always agree with. Rather than pulling rank, he uses the phrase "Disagree but commit", making clear he does not agree with the decision but now it is made, he will put everything behind making the proposed solution work.

Both these techniques illustrate important elements of leading with vision and values. Pushing decision making down into the organisation brings it closer to the customer and is, therefore, more likely to result in decisions that better reflect their needs. It also speeds up the decision-making process, as layers of approval are removed. To extend Bill Gore's analogy, the fastest vessels skim across the water with most of their structure out of the water: the Plimsoll line is just above the propellor. The bright people you have hired want to contribute; they want the opportunity to shape their work and the organisation. Leading with vision and values gives them the opportunity to bring their perspective to the party, which not only increases your organisation's decision-making capability but increases engagement. This engagement and the conversations that underpin it bring diverse inputs to test and enrich the vision and values; a process which further increases understanding. You are on the way to creating a virtuous circle with the power to drive innovation and execution.

It starts with you

The CEO of a large customer once told me that organisations are shadows of their leaders. You will never create a customer-focused business if you do not embody the underlying principles and are seen to embed them in the decisions and actions you take. Remember the words of Ralph Waldo Emerson: *"Your actions speak so loudly, I cannot hear what you are saying."* It was not until I was a CEO myself that I truly understood this. *Communiaction* (no, it's not misspelled; read it again), what you do, is the most powerful tool you have. Your actions underpin your integrity, trust and reputation, all of which are at the heart of leadership. It's personal, and if it's not, it won't work.

Weaving the customer's perspective into all your communications is a good starting point. I am a great believer in the power of shared visions. In the later years of Clicktools, the quarterly all hands update was built around our vision picture. Performance was communicated as an overlay of the key metrics, followed by overlays setting out the quarter's progress on key initiatives and the areas of focus for the next quarter. Customers were at the core of our vision, so were centre stage in our communications and our actions. This approach reinforced the vision, building coherence between words and deeds.

You have to be the cheerleader for the customer, not just by extolling the importance of a united focus on value for customers but by driving the actions that deliver and maintain it. You have to be the one to drive the requirement for a company-wide ICP. You have to be the one always asking, "How does this affect our chosen customers?" You have to be the one looking beyond the departmental silos and cajoling people to think about what is right for the customer and the business, not just their own team. You must be the one seeking out measures and programmes that unite the organisation behind its quest for converting value to customers into revenue for your company.

Artefacts can be a very simple but effective way of reinforcing focus on the customer. Jeff Bezos famously has an empty chair at meetings, representing the customer. At Virgin Money, Managing Director Jayne-Anne Gadhia always asked how their decisions would shape the discussion around the customer's kitchen table. One company named its meeting rooms after long-term customers. On their own these are gimmicks, but as one element of a concerted effort to drive customer focus, they play a useful role, constantly reminding people why the company exists.

If you really want to build an organisation that delivers great value for customers and great results for your company, start with one simple thing. Each morning, look in the mirror and ask yourself, "Do I want it?"

It's personal!

Index

I

J

M

N

O

organisation design · 29, 30, 38, 44, 57, 58, 59, 64, 70, 102, 108
outcome · 25, 35, 37, 42, 72, 73, 82, 85, 86, 87, 88, 90, 93, 99, 101, 105, 110,
    123, 124
outside-in design · 59, 64

P

Paul Henderson · 85, 93
performance-based pricing · 129
Peter Drucker · 16
pipeline · 98, 102, 137
product-enabled value · 85, 114, 119, 121, 125, 126, 127, 129
product-led · 33, 53, 98, 99, 114, 118, 120
Profitwell · 32
psychology · 34, 36, 72, 76, 78, 79, 88, 123, 124, 128, 130
purpose · 33, 43, 58, 59, 60, 61, 62, 64, 66, 67, 68, 70, 88, 101, 114, 115,
    117, 130, 138

R

Rahul Vohra · 126
Rav Dhaliwal · 19, 37, 48, 96, 98
referrals · 49, 67
ROI · 72, 73, 86
role profile · 64, 73, 74, 76, 80, 132

S

sales · 25, 26, 31, 33, 36, 37, 40, 41, 48, 49, 51, 52, 53, 54, 56, 57, 62, 65, 66,
    72, 73, 81, 85, 90, 95, 96, 97, 98, 99, 100, 101, 102, 119, 122, 127, 132
Salesforce · 14, 15, 134, 135
scientific management · 42, 44
segmentation · 27, 28, 103, 106, 108
self-service · 39, 104, 105, 107, 116, 119, 120
single customer view · 110, 111, 134
success by design · 38, 57, 138
success plan · 26, 36, 37, 63, 86, 90, 93, 120, 122, 124, 126
Survey Monkey · 14, 19, 117, 120, 147

T

V

About the Author

Following an eclectic career including logistics, management development, academia and consulting, David founded Clicktools in 2000 – one of the UK's first B2B SaaS companies. As CEO, he bootstrapped growth and led the company through two liquidity events, selling 49.9% to Survey Monkey in 2010 before selling 100% to Callidus Cloud in 2014.

In 2015, David founded TheCustomer.Co to advise B2B SaaS companies and investors on converting value for customers into growth by building company-wide capabilities. He consults with and coaches CEOs and leadership teams of companies globally that share his passion for customer-led growth and are willing to question common practice.

In 2020, David founded the Customer Success Leadership Institute to help build the contribution and effectiveness of this important capability.

In his spare time, David likes to think and write and, above all, spend time with family, preferably over a good meal and fine wine.

https://thecustomer.co

https://www.linkedin.com/in/davidjacksonuk

Also by David Jackson

Dynamic organisations: the challenge of change

Organisations around the world are in crisis! The principles and approaches on which success is built are no longer clear. Success in the future will require challenging many of the concepts and practices which underpin most organisations today. David Jackson provides practical advice, supported by case studies, for managers seeking to build "dynamic organisations" where customers drive continuous improvement and people are challenged by clear and incisive leadership.

Published 1997

Becoming Dynamic: Creating and sustaining the Dynamic Organisation

In this follow-up to the ground-breaking *Dynamic Organisations*, David Jackson leads the reader step-by-step through the change management process. Jackson wrote *Becoming Dynamic* to communicate the lessons he has learnt after many years of working as a consultant with senior managers struggling to make change work in a variety of companies. This is reflected in his spirited and enthusiastic style and his refreshing culture, learning and performance.

Published 2000

Printed in Great Britain
by Amazon